180 DAYS™ of Reading for Fourth Grade

Unit 4
WEEK 3
DAY
4–5

Name: ______________________ Date: ______________

As You Read

Circle five words that help tell the story's plot.

Making the Team

Kyle sat glumly on his bed, ignoring the fact that he needed to tie his shoes and get downstairs so Dad could take him to swim team tryouts. He loved swimming, but he was convinced he wouldn't be fast enough to impress the coach—not without fins at least. He always wore fins when he swam in the ocean, and he really didn't want to embarrass himself in front of the coach. Kyle heard [illegible] coming up the staircase, and Dad poked

[illegible] asked, sitting down next to [illegible] ming."

[illegible] shoulders, unsure of what to say.

[illegible] et me guess—you're afraid you won't make the team, right?" Dad asked.

Kyle glanced up with surprise. How had he guessed?

"Listen," Dad said. "I know you're probably scared, but why not at least [illegible] the coach time you? There's nothing to lose by trying, even if you don't end [illegible] making the team. And who knows—you might even surprise yourself."

Kyle thought for a moment, weighing his options. "That makes sense," he [illegible] "Okay, I guess I'll go. Thanks, Dad."

[illegible] an hour later, Kyle was anxiously waiting with everyone else who [illegible] to try out. He tried to bring back that excited feeling he had when [illegible] first heard about the swim team tryouts. Then, the coach called his name [illegible] Kyle almost froze, but he forced himself to the edge of the swimming po[illegible] Time seemed to slow down, and all Kyle focused on was his breathing a[illegible] the sparkling water below. The coach blew his whistle and Kyle plunged [illegible] [illegible]g through the water as quickly as he could. When he reached the [illegible] [illegible] the pool, he popped up and grasped the steel ladder at the pool's ed[illegible] dripping hair out of his eyes. He climbed out of the water and [illegible] where the coach was standing.

[illegible] squinted at his stopwatch and then smiled at Kyle.

[illegible] terrific time!" he said, clapping Kyle on the back. "In fact, yo[illegible] fastest times I've seen today. You're like a fish, and you'll do [illegible] the swim team."

135046—180 Days of

Authors

Kristin Kemp, M.A.Ed.

Curtis Slepian

Program Credits

Corinne Burton, M.A.Ed., *President* and *Publisher*
Emily R. Smith, M.A.Ed., *SVP of Content Development*
Véronique Bos, *Vice President of Creative*
Lynette Ordoñez, *Content Manager*
Ashley Oberhaus, M.Ed., *Content Specialist*
Melissa Laughlin, *Editor*
David Slayton, *Assistant Editor*
Jill Malcolm, *Graphic Designer*

Image Credits: p.23 Getty Images/Patrick Riviere/Staff; p.59 (top left) Shutterstock/possohh; p.59 Shutterstock/Bill Morson; p.65 (bottom right) Shutterstock/Cintia Erdens Paiva; p.67 Shutterstock/Celso Pupo; p.84 Wikimedia/Daisy Moore Archive; p.104 Shutterstock/Vintagepix; p.122 Shutterstock/Rey Rodriguez; p.140 Wikimedia/National Portrait Gallery; p.193 Wikimedia/David Levy; all other images from Shutterstock and/or iStock

Standards

A division of Teacher Created Materials
5482 Argosy Avenue
Huntington Beach, CA 92649
www.tcmpub.com/shell-education
ISBN 979-8-7659-1806-7

Printed in China 51497

Table of Contents

Introduction

The Need for Practice

To be successful in today's reading classroom, students must deeply understand both concepts and procedures so that they can discuss and demonstrate their understanding. Demonstrating understanding is a process that must be continually practiced for students to be successful. According to Robert Marzano, "Practice has always been, and always will be, a necessary ingredient to learning procedural knowledge at a level at which students execute it independently" (2010, 83). Practice is especially important to help students apply reading comprehension strategies and word-study skills. *180 Days of Reading* offers teachers and parents a full page of reading comprehension and word recognition practice activities for each day of the school year.

The Science of Reading

For some people, reading comes easily. They barely remember how it happened. For others, learning to read takes more effort.

The goal of reading research is to understand the differences in how people learn to read and find the best ways to help all students learn. The term *Science of Reading* is commonly used to refer to this body of research. It helps people understand how to provide instruction in learning the code of the English language, how to develop fluency, and how to navigate challenging text and make sense of it.

Much of this research has been around for decades. In fact, in the late 1990s, Congress commissioned a review of the reading research. In 2000, the National Reading Panel (NRP) published a report that became the backbone of the Science of Reading. The NRP report highlights five components of effective reading instruction. These include the following:

- **Phonemic Awareness:** understanding and manipulating individual speech sounds
- **Phonics:** matching sounds to letters for use in reading and spelling
- **Fluency:** reading connected text accurately and smoothly
- **Vocabulary:** knowing the meanings of words in speech and in print
- **Reading Comprehension:** understanding what is read

There are two commonly referenced frameworks that build on reading research and provide a visual way for people to understand what is needed to learn to read. In the mid-1980s, a framework called the Simple View of Reading was introduced (Gough and Tunmer 1986). It shows that reading comprehension is possible when students are able to decode (or read) the words and have the language to understand the words.

The Simple View of Reading

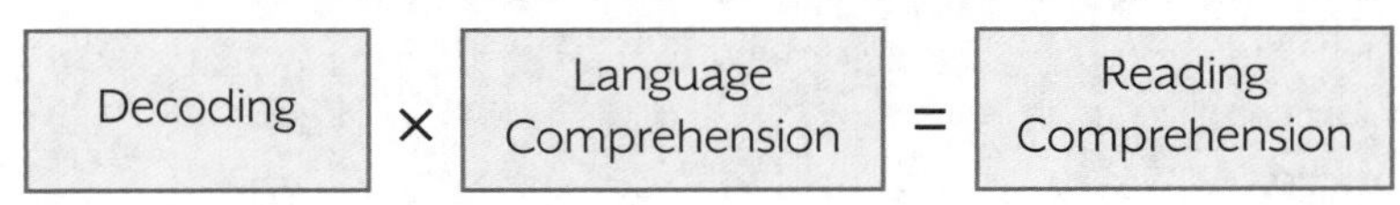

Another framework that builds on the research behind the Science of Reading is Scarborough's Reading Rope (Scarborough 2001). It shows specific skills needed for both language comprehension and word recognition. The "strands" of the rope for language comprehension include having background content knowledge, knowing vocabulary, understanding language structure, having verbal reasoning, and understanding literacy. Word recognition includes phonological awareness, decoding skills, and sight recognition of familiar words (Scarborough 2001). As individual skills are strengthened and practiced, they become increasingly strategic and automatic to promote reading comprehension.

The Science of Reading *(cont.)*

Many parts of our understanding of how people learn to read stand the test of time and have been confirmed by more recent studies. However, new research continues to add to the understanding of reading. Some of this research shows the importance of wide reading (reading about a variety of topics), motivation, and self-regulation. The conversation will never be over, as new research will continue to refine the understanding of how people learn to read. There is always more to learn!

180 Days of Reading has been informed by this reading research. This series provides opportunities for students to practice the skills that years of research indicate contribute to reading growth. There are several features in this book that are supported by the Science of Reading.

Text Selection

- Carefully chosen texts offer experiences in a **wide range of text types**. Each unit includes nonfiction, fiction, and a nontraditional text type or genre (e.g., letters, newspaper articles, advertisements, menus).
- Texts intentionally build upon one another to help students **build background knowledge** from day to day.
- Engaging with texts on the same topic for a thematic unit enables students to become familiar with related **vocabulary**, **language structure**, and **literacy knowledge**. This allows reading to become increasingly strategic and automatic, leading to better **fluency** and **comprehension**.

Activity Design

- Specific **language comprehension** and **word-recognition skills** are reinforced throughout the activities.
- Each text includes a purpose for reading and an opportunity to practice various reading strategies through annotation. This promotes **close reading** of the text.
- Paired fiction and nonfiction texts are used to promote **comparison** and encourage students to **make connections** between texts within a unit.
- Students **write to demonstrate understanding** of the texts. Students provide written responses in a variety of forms, including short answers, open-ended responses, and creating their own versions of nontraditional texts.

This book provides the regular practice of reading skills that students need as they develop into excellent readers.

How to Use This Resource

Unit Structure Overview

This resource is organized into 12 units. Each three-week unit is organized in a consistent format for ease of use.

Week 1: Nonfiction

Day 1	Students read nonfiction text and answer multiple-choice questions.
Day 2	Students read nonfiction text and answer multiple-choice questions.
Day 3	Students read nonfiction text and answer multiple-choice, short answer, and open response questions.
Day 4	Students read longer nonfiction text, answer multiple-choice questions, and complete graphic organizers.
Day 5	Students reread the text from Day 4 and answer reading response questions.

Week 2: Fiction

Day 1	Students read fiction text and answer multiple-choice questions.
Day 2	Students read fiction text and answer multiple-choice questions.
Day 3	Students read fiction text and answer multiple-choice, short answer, and constructed response questions.
Day 4	Students read longer fiction text, answer multiple-choice questions, and complete graphic organizers.
Day 5	Students reread the text from Day 4 and answer reading response questions.

Week 3: Nontraditional Text

Day 1	Students read nontraditional text and answer multiple-choice and open response questions.
Day 2	Students complete close reading activities with paired text from the unit.
Day 3	Students complete close reading activities with paired text from the unit.
Day 4	Students write responses to prompts that have them connect and reflect on different genres of texts from this unit.
Day 5	Students write their own versions of the nontraditional text from Day 1 of this week.

How to Use This Resource *(cont.)*

Unit Structure Overview *(cont.)*

Paired Texts

State standards have brought into focus the importance of preparing students for college and career success by expanding their critical-thinking and analytical skills. It is no longer enough for students to read and comprehend a single text on a topic. Rather, the integration of ideas across texts is crucial for a more comprehensive understanding of themes presented by authors.

Literacy specialist Jennifer Soalt has written that paired texts are "uniquely suited to scaffolding and extending students' comprehension" (2005, 680). She identifies three ways in which paired fiction and nonfiction are particularly effective in increasing comprehension: the building of background knowledge, the development of vocabulary, and the increase in student motivation (Soalt 2005).

Each three-week unit in *180 Days of Reading* is connected by a common theme or topic. Packets of each week's or each unit's practice pages can be prepared for students.

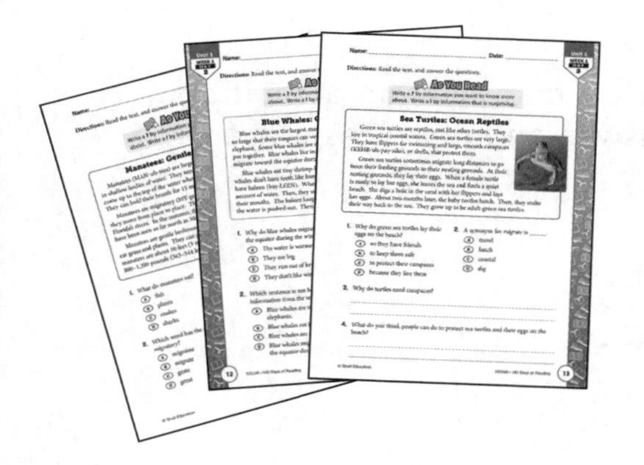

During Week 1, students read nonfictional texts and answer questions.

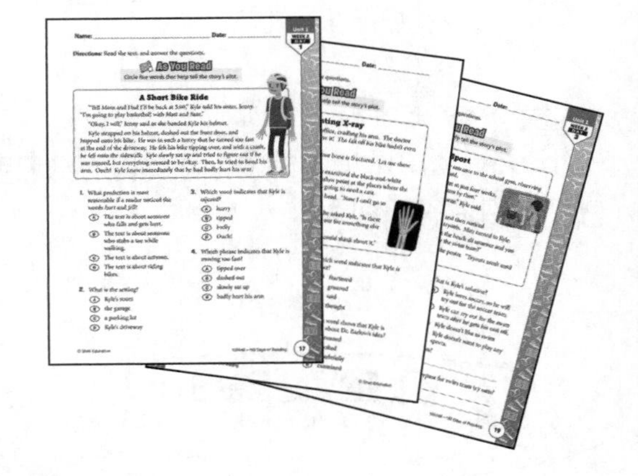

During Week 2, students read fictional texts and answer questions.

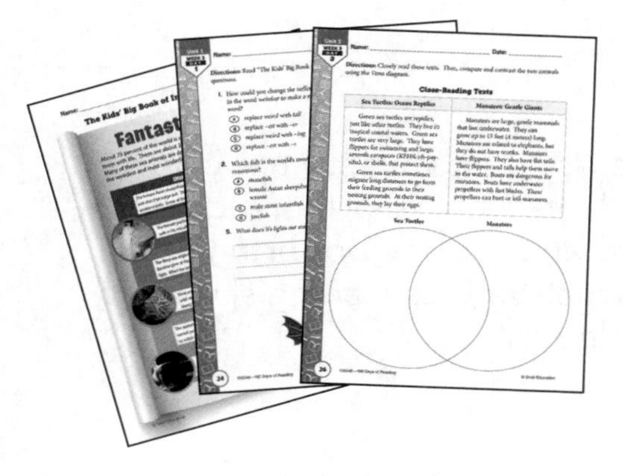

During Week 3, students read nontraditional texts (advertisements, poems, letters, etc.), answer questions, and complete close reading and writing activities.

How to Use This Resource *(cont.)*

Student Practice Pages

Practice pages reinforce grade-level skills across a variety of reading concepts for each day of the school year. Each day's reading activity is provided as a full practice page, making them easy to prepare and implement as part of a morning routine, at the beginning of each reading lesson, or as homework.

Practice Pages for Weeks 1 and 2

Days 1 and 2 of each week follow a consistent format, with a short text passage and multiple-choice questions.

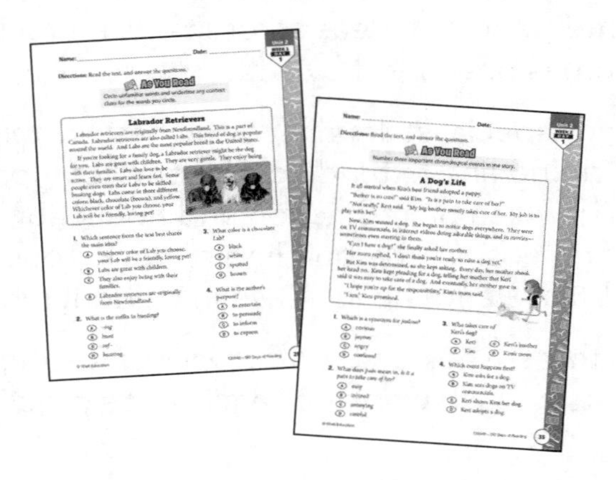

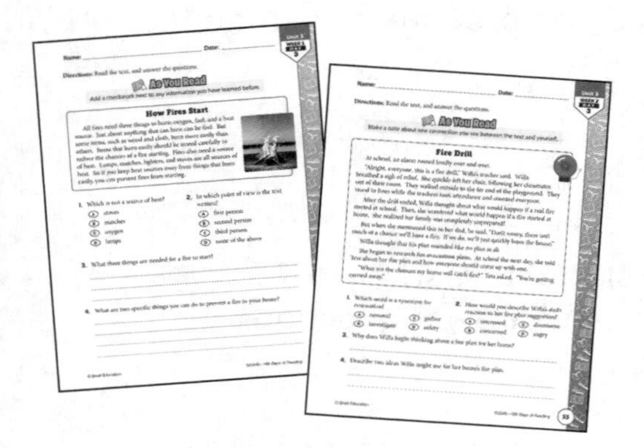

Days 3 and 4 have a combination of multiple-choice, short-answer, and open-response questions.

On day 5, students complete text-based writing prompts.

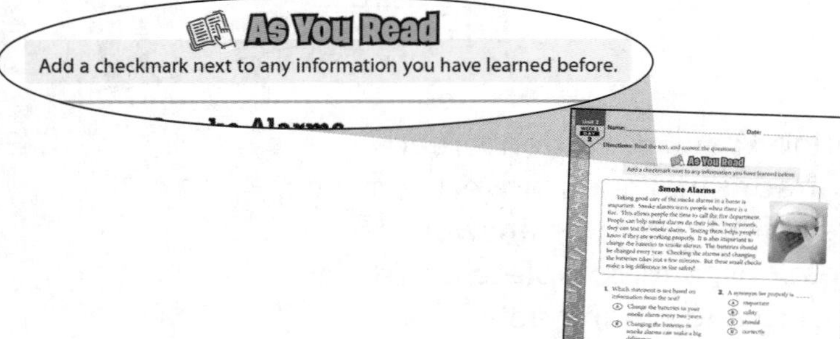

The As You Read activities give students a purpose for reading the texts and provide opportunities to practice various reading skills and strategies.

How to Use This Resource

Student Practice Pages *(cont.)*

Practice Page For Weeks 3

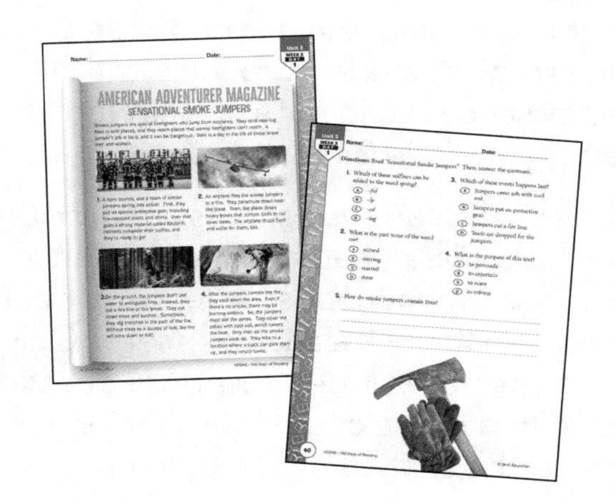
AMERICAN ADVENTURER MAGAZINE

SENSATIONAL SMOKE JUMPERS

Day 1 of this week follows a consistent format, with a nontraditional text and multiple-choice and constructed response questions.

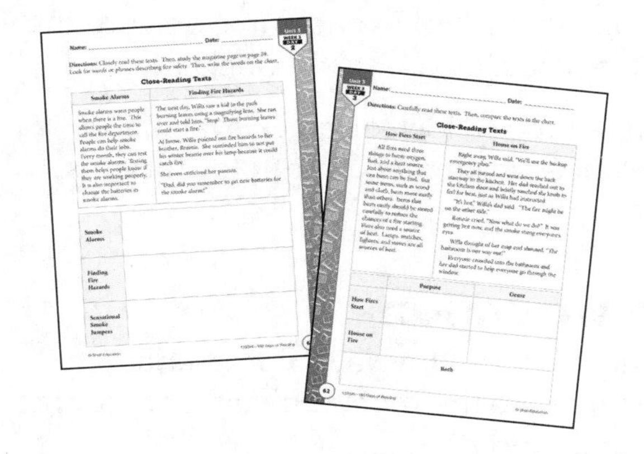
Close-Reading Texts

On days 2 and 3, students engage in close reading activities of paired texts. Students are encouraged to compare and contrast different aspects of the texts they read in the entire unit.

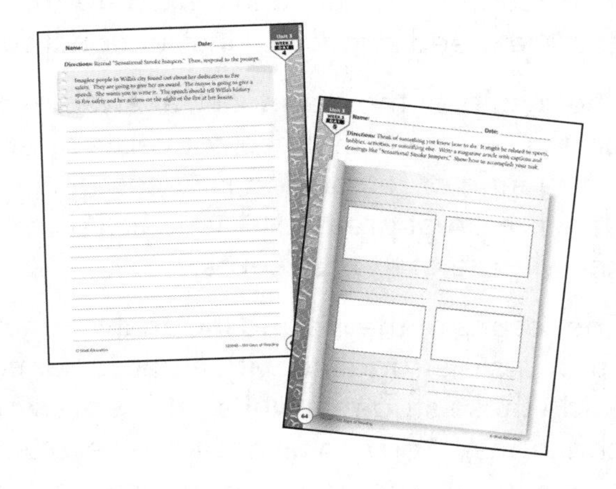

On days 4 and 5, students think about the texts in the entire unit, respond to writing prompts, and construct their own versions of diverse texts. Students are encouraged to use information from texts throughout the unit to inspire and support their writing.

Instructional Options

180 Days of Reading is a flexible resource that can be used in various instructional settings for different purposes.

- Use these student pages as daily warm-up activities or as review.
- Work with students in small groups, allowing them to focus on specific skills. This setting also lends itself to partner and group discussions about the texts.
- Student pages in this resource can be completed independently during center times and as activities for early finishers.

How to Use This Resource *(cont.)*

Diagnostic Assessment

The practice pages in this book can be used as diagnostic assessments. These activity pages require students to think critically, respond to text-dependent questions, and utilize reading and writing skills and strategies. (An answer key for the practice pages is provided starting on page 230.)

For each unit, analysis sheets are provided as *Microsoft Word®* files in the digital resources. There is a *Class Analysis Sheet* and an *Individual Analysis Sheet*. Use the file that matches your assessment needs. After each week, record how many answers each student got correct on the unit's analysis sheet. Only record the answers for the multiple-choice questions. The written-response questions and graphic organizers can be evaluated using the writing rubric or other evaluation tools (see below). At the end of each unit, analyze the data on the analysis sheet to determine instructional focuses for your child or class.

The diagnostic analysis tools included in the digital resources allow for quick evaluation and ongoing monitoring of student work. See at a glance which reading genre students may need to focus on further to develop proficiency.

Using the Results to Differentiate Instruction

Once results are gathered and analyzed, use the data to inform the way to differentiate instruction. The data can help determine which concepts are the most difficult for students and that need additional instructional support and continued practice.

The results of the diagnostic analysis may show that an entire class is struggling with a particular genre. If these concepts have been taught in the past, this indicates that further instruction or reteaching is necessary. If these concepts have not been taught yet, this data is a great preassessment and demonstrates that students do not have a working knowledge of the concepts.

The results of the diagnostic analysis may also show that an individual or small group of students is struggling with a particular concept or group of concepts. Consider pulling aside these students while others are working independently to instruct further on the concept(s). You can also use the results to help identify individuals or groups of proficient students who are ready for enrichment or above-grade-level instruction. These students may benefit from independent learning contracts or more challenging activities.

Writing Rubric

A rubric for written responses is provided on page 229. Display the rubric for students to reference as they write. Score students' written responses, and provide them with feedback on their writing.

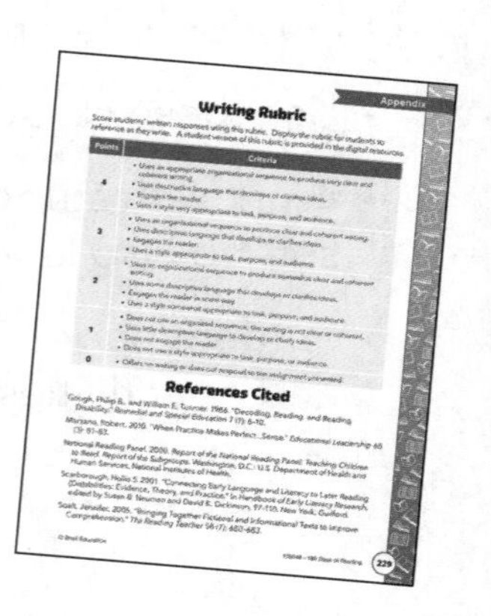
Writing Rubric

References Cited

Name: ______________________ Date: ______________

Directions: Read the text, and answer the questions.

Write a **?** by information you want to know more about. Write a **!** by information that is surprising.

Manatees: Gentle Giants

Manatees (MAN-uh-tees) are large mammals. They live in shallow bodies of water. They need to breathe air. They come up to the top of the water when they need more air. They can hold their breath for 15 minutes!

Manatees are migratory (MY-gruh-tor-ee). This means they move from place to place. They spend winters in Florida's rivers. In the summer, they move northwest. They have been seen as far north as Massachusetts!

Manatees are gentle herbivores (HUHR-buh-vorz). They eat grass and plants. They can grow to be very large. Adult manatees are about 10 feet (3 meters) long. They weigh 800–1,200 pounds (363–544 kilograms). That's about the size of a small bus!

1. What do manatees eat?
   - (A) fish
   - (B) plants
   - (C) snakes
   - (D) sharks

2. Which word has the same root as *migratory*?
   - (A) migraine
   - (B) migrate
   - (C) grate
   - (D) great

3. Migratory animals are animals that _____.
   - (A) move from one place to another
   - (B) eat other animals
   - (C) stay in one place all year long
   - (D) eat grass and plants

4. What type of text would have a similar tone?
   - (A) a history book
   - (B) a science-fiction novel
   - (C) a science textbook
   - (D) a travel magazine

Name: ______________________________ Date: ________________

Directions: Read the text, and answer the questions.

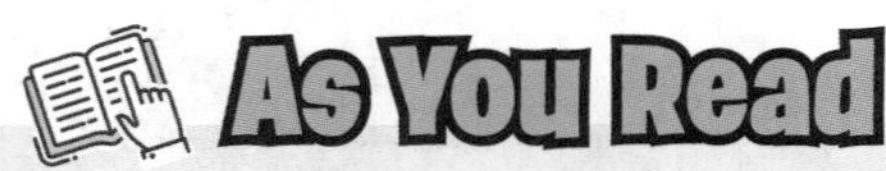

Write a **?** by information you want to know more about. Write a **!** by information that is surprising.

Blue Whales: Ocean Giants

Blue whales are the largest mammals on Earth. They are so large that their tongues can weigh nearly as much as a small elephant. Some blue whales are as long as three school buses put together. Blue whales live in every ocean on Earth, and they migrate toward the equator during the winter.

Blue whales eat tiny shrimp-like animals called krill. Blue whales don't have teeth like humans do. Instead, blue whales have baleen (bay-LEEN). When blue whales are hungry, they swallow a large amount of water. Then, they use their huge tongues to force the water out of their mouths. The baleen keeps the krill inside their mouths while the rest of the water is pushed out. Then, they can swallow their food.

1. Why do blue whales migrate toward the equator during the winter?
   - (A) The water is warmer there.
   - (B) They are big.
   - (C) They run out of krill.
   - (D) They don't like winter.

2. Which sentence is **not** based on information from the text?
   - (A) Blue whales are smaller than elephants.
   - (B) Blue whales eat krill.
   - (C) Blue whales are mammals.
   - (D) Blue whales migrate during the winter.

3. What does the suffix –est in the word *largest* mean?
   - (A) the most
   - (B) the least
   - (C) already happened
   - (D) belonging to

4. Which definition of *live* is used in this sentence from the text?
   They live in every ocean on Earth...
   - (A) current
   - (B) inhabit
   - (C) in person
   - (D) stay

Name: ______________________________ Date: ______________

Directions: Read the text, and answer the questions.

Write a **?** by information you want to know more about. Write a **!** by information that is surprising.

Sea Turtles: Ocean Reptiles

Green sea turtles are reptiles, just like other turtles. They live in tropical coastal waters. Green sea turtles are very large. They have flippers for swimming and large, smooth carapaces (KEHR-uh-pay-sihs), or shells, that protect them.

Green sea turtles sometimes migrate long distances to go from their feeding grounds to their nesting grounds. At their nesting grounds, they lay their eggs. When a female turtle is ready to lay her eggs, she leaves the sea and finds a quiet beach. She digs a hole in the sand with her flippers and lays her eggs. About two months later, the baby turtles hatch. Then, they make their way back to the sea. They grow up to be adult green sea turtles.

1. Where do green sea turtles lay their eggs?
   - (A) underwater
   - (B) in a hole in the sand
   - (C) next to large rocks
   - (D) in a coral reef

2. A synonym for *migrate* is _____.
   - (A) travel
   - (B) hatch
   - (C) coastal
   - (D) dig

3. Why do turtles need carapaces?

____

____

4. What do you think people can do to protect sea turtles and their eggs on the beach?

____

____

Name: ______________________________ Date: ________________

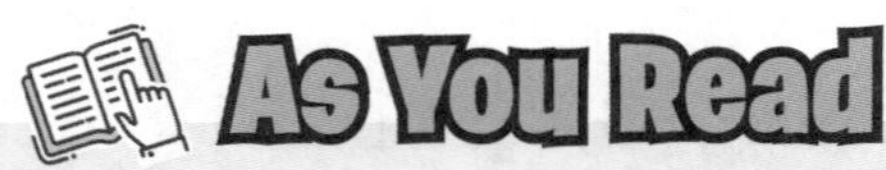

Write a **?** by information you want to know more about.
Write a **!** by information that is surprising.

A World Under the Water

Some animals know how to swim from the time they are born. This is because they live underwater, and they have to be able to swim to survive. Many different kinds of animals live underwater. They all face challenges from humans.

Manatees are large, gentle mammals that live underwater. They can grow up to 13 feet (4 meters) long. Manatees are related to elephants, but they do not have trunks. Manatees have flippers. They also have flat tails. Their flippers and tails help them move in the water. Boats are dangerous for manatees. Boats have underwater propellers with fast blades. These propellers can hurt or kill manatees.

Blue whales are the largest underwater mammals on Earth. An adult blue whale is about the size of a large airplane! Blue whales eat a kind of shrimp called krill. They use the baleen in their mouths to filter them out of the water. In the past, people used to hunt blue whales for their resources. Blue whales almost became extinct. People used whale oil for many uses, including cooking and lamp lighting. They used baleen because it was light but strong. It took time, but laws were made to protect blue whales. Now, most countries do not allow blue whale hunting.

Green sea turtles live underwater, too. But they are not mammals. Green sea turtles are reptiles. They live in warm coastal waters. Green sea turtles eat plants that grow underwater. Some green sea turtles come out of the water to warm up on dry land. Female green sea turtles also come out of the water to lay their eggs. When the babies are born, they make their way back to the sea. Later, those turtles have babies of their own. People kill green sea turtles for their meat and their eggs. Boats and fishing nets can also hurt green sea turtles.

Manatees, blue whales, and green sea turtles are just a few of the wonderful sea animals living underwater. They all face many dangers from humans. But they are able to overcome them and live peacefully underwater.

Name: ______________________ Date: ____________

Directions: Read "A World Under the Water." Then, answer the questions.

1. The author most likely wrote the text to ______.

- (A) tell about animals that live underwater
- (B) get you to go swimming
- (C) tell how to catch a manatee
- (D) tell about ocean plant life

2. How are manatees and blue whales alike?

- (A) They both eat krill.
- (B) They are both the size of an airplane.
- (C) They are both mammals.
- (D) They are both related to elephants.

3. Which keywords are most important to the text?

- (A) *gentle, flippers,* and *boats*
- (B) *water, airplane,* and *coastal*
- (C) *manatees, whales,* and *turtles*
- (D) *elephants, oil,* and *mammals*

4. What is the main idea of the text?

- (A) Manatees, blue whales, and green sea turtles are all sea animals that face dangers from humans.
- (B) Blue whales were almost extinct, so laws were made to protect them.
- (C) Green sea turtles live in warm coastal areas and lay eggs on the beach.
- (D) Boat propellers can hurt or kill manatees.

5. Choose two animals from the passage. Use a Venn diagram to compare and contrast them.

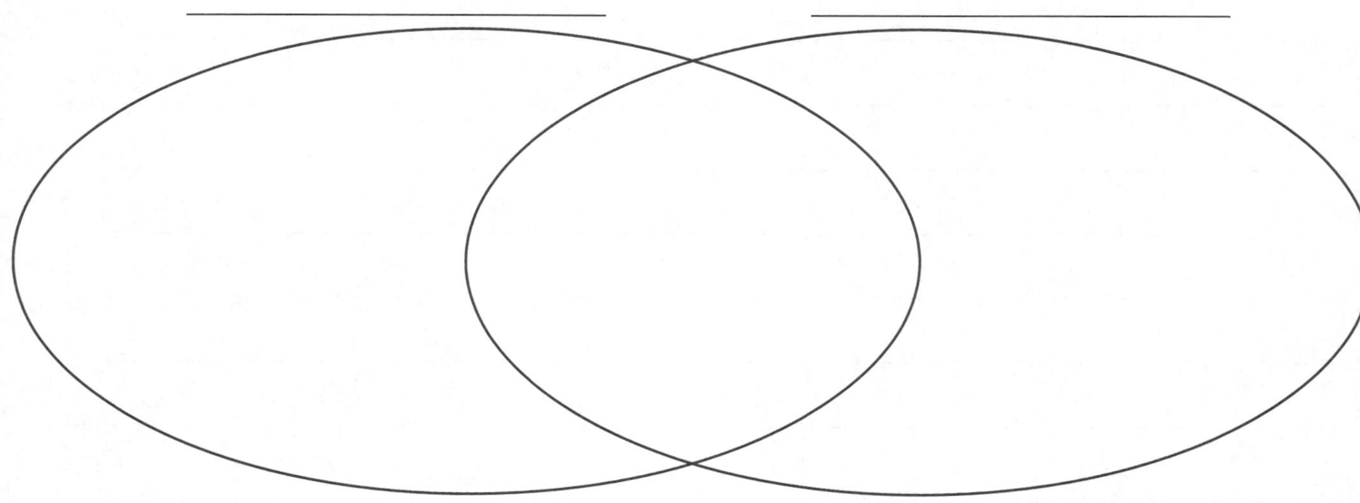

Unit 1
WEEK 1
DAY
5

Name: ______________________________ Date: ______________

Directions: Reread "A World Under the Water." Then, respond to the prompt.

Manatees, blue whales, and sea turtles all face danger from humans. Write a paragraph to summarize the dangers each animal faces and what people can do to help. Don't forget an introduction and a conclusion sentence.

Name: ______________________ Date: ____________

Directions: Read the text, and answer the questions.

Circle five words that help tell the story's plot.

A Short Bike Ride

"Tell Mom and Dad I'll be back at 5:00," Kyle told his sister, Jenny. "I'm going to play basketball with Matt and Sam."

"Okay, I will," Jenny said as she handed Kyle his helmet.

Kyle strapped on his helmet, dashed out the front door, and hopped onto his bike. He was in such a hurry that he turned too fast at the end of the driveway. He felt his bike tipping over, and with a crash, he fell onto the sidewalk. Kyle slowly sat up and tried to figure out if he was injured, but everything seemed to be okay. Then, he tried to bend his arm. Ouch! Kyle knew immediately that he had badly hurt his arm.

1. What prediction is most reasonable if a reader noticed the words *hurt* and *fell*?
   - (A) The text is about someone who falls and gets hurt.
   - (B) The text is about someone who gets sick.
   - (C) The text is about autumn.
   - (D) The text is about riding bikes.

2. What is the setting?
   - (A) Kyle's room
   - (B) the garage
   - (C) a parking lot
   - (D) Kyle's driveway

3. Which word indicates that Kyle is injured?
   - (A) hurry
   - (B) tipped
   - (C) badly
   - (D) Ouch!

4. Which phrase indicates that Kyle is moving too fast?
   - (A) tipped over
   - (B) dashed out
   - (C) slowly sat up
   - (D) badly hurt his arm

Name: ______________________________ Date: ________________

Directions: Read the text, and answer the questions.

Circle five words that help tell the story's plot.

A Disappointing X-ray

Kyle groaned as he sat in the doctor's office, cradling his arm. The doctor said it was broken, and Kyle couldn't believe it! The fall off his bike hadn't even been that bad.

"I'm very sorry," said Dr. Barlow, "but your bone is fractured. Let me show you the X-ray we took."

Dr. Barlow carefully showed Kyle how he examined the black-and-white X-ray. Kyle's spirits fell as he watched Dr. Barlow point at the places where the bone was fractured, and Kyle realized he was going to need a cast.

"This isn't fair!" Kyle moaned, shaking his head. "Now I can't go to baseball tryouts next week."

Dr. Barlow thought for a minute, and then he asked Kyle, "Is there another sport you enjoy? Maybe you could try out for something else after your arm heals."

"Maybe," Kyle said doubtfully, "but I guess I could think about it."

1. What is Dr. Barlow's solution?
   - (A) Kyle should get another X-ray.
   - (B) Kyle should ride his bike more.
   - (C) Kyle should try out for baseball.
   - (D) Kyle should try another sport.

2. Which synonym for *fractured* is used in the text?
   - (A) broken
   - (B) bitten
   - (C) healed
   - (D) covered

3. Which word indicates that Kyle is upset?
   - (A) fractured
   - (B) groaned
   - (C) said
   - (D) thought

4. Which word shows that Kyle is unsure about Dr. Barlow's idea?
   - (A) thought
   - (B) looked
   - (C) doubtfully
   - (D) examined

Name: ______________________________ Date: ________________

Directions: Read the text, and answer the questions.

Circle five words that help tell the story's plot.

A New Sport

Kyle and his best friend Matt stood by the entrance to the school gym, observing a list of sports tryout dates on the bulletin board.

"Here's one," Matt said. "Soccer tryouts start in just four weeks, so you won't have that annoying cast on your arm by then."

"Soccer's okay, but it's definitely not my favorite," Kyle said. "Let's see if anything else seems interesting."

Matt and Kyle scanned the rest of the poster and then noticed another sign to the right advertising swim team tryouts. Matt turned to Kyle.

"You like to swim, Kyle," Matt said. "You're at the beach all summer and you basically live in the ocean. You should try out for the swim team!"

"Maybe I will," Kyle replied, looking closer at the poster. "Tryouts aren't until next month."

1. How does Kyle feel about soccer?

- (A) He thinks it is fun.
- (B) He wants to try out for the soccer team.
- (C) He thinks it's just okay.
- (D) He doesn't want to play the same sport as Matt.

2. What is Kyle's solution?

- (A) Kyle loves soccer, so he will try out for the soccer team.
- (B) Kyle can try out for the swim team after he gets his cast off.
- (C) Kyle doesn't like to swim.
- (D) Kyle doesn't want to play any sports.

3. Why will Kyle be able to try out for the swim team?

____

4. What advice would you give to Kyle to help him prepare for swim team try outs?

____

____

Name: ______________________ Date: ______________

Circle five words that help tell the story's plot.

Making the Team

Kyle sat glumly on his bed, ignoring the fact that he needed to tie his shoes and get downstairs so Dad could take him to swim team tryouts. He loved swimming, but he was convinced he wouldn't be fast enough to impress the coach—not without fins at least. He always wore fins when he swam in the ocean, and he really didn't want to embarrass himself in front of the coach. Kyle heard heavy footsteps coming up the staircase, and Dad poked his head into Kyle's room.

"What's up, Kyle?" Dad asked, sitting down next to him. "I thought you enjoyed swimming."

Kyle shrugged his shoulders, unsure of what to say.

"Let me guess—you're afraid you won't make the team, right?" Dad asked.

Kyle glanced up with surprise. How had he guessed?

"Listen," Dad said. "I know you're probably scared, but why not at least have the coach time you? There's nothing to lose by trying, even if you don't end up making the team. And who knows—you might even surprise yourself."

Kyle thought for a moment, weighing his options. "That makes sense," he sighed. "Okay, I guess I'll go. Thanks, Dad."

Half an hour later, Kyle was anxiously waiting with everyone else who wanted to try out. He tried to bring back that excited feeling he had when he first heard about the swim team tryouts. Then, the coach called his name, and Kyle almost froze, but he forced himself to the edge of the swimming pool. Time seemed to slow down, and all Kyle focused on was his breathing and the sparkling water below. The coach blew his whistle and Kyle plunged in, churning through the water as quickly as he could. When he reached the other side of the pool, he popped up and grasped the steel ladder at the pool's edge, shaking his dripping hair out of his eyes. He climbed out of the water and returned to where the coach was standing.

The coach squinted at his stopwatch and then smiled at Kyle.

"You had a terrific time!" he said, clapping Kyle on the back. "In fact, you got one of the fastest times I've seen today. You're like a fish, and you'll do a fantastic job on the swim team."

Name: ______________________________ Date: ______________

Directions: Read "Making the Team." Then, answer the questions.

1. What is the problem?

(A) Kyle is afraid he will hurt himself.

(B) Kyle can't find his swimsuit.

(C) Kyle won't listen to his father.

(D) Kyle is afraid he won't make the team.

2. Kyle's experience is most like that of someone who ______.

(A) wins the lottery

(B) forgets to study for a test and fails

(C) is nervous about a test but gets a good grade

(D) lets down a family member

3. What is the author's purpose?

(A) to entertain readers with a story

(B) to persuade readers to try out for a swim team

(C) to teach readers how to play water polo

(D) to explain how to swim

4. Which sentence is the most climactic moment in the text?

(A) He loved swimming, but he was convinced he wouldn't be fast enough to impress the coach—not without fins at least.

(B) Dad poked his head into Kyle's room.

(C) Then, the coach called his name, and Kyle almost froze, but he forced himself to the edge of the swimming pool.

(D) Kyle heard heavy footsteps coming up the staircase, and Dad poked his head into Kyle's room.

5. Write five important events in the story in chronological order.

1.	
2.	
3.	
4.	
5.	

Name: ______________________________ Date: ______________

Directions: Reread "Making the Team." Then, respond to the prompt.

Add to the story. Write what you think will happen next. Use some dialogue in your new part of the story. Add an illustration to go with your writing.

Fantastic Fish!

About 75 percent of the world is covered by water. These oceans teem with life. There are about 230,000 species that we know of. Many of these sea animals are downright unusual. Here are some of the weirdest and most wonderful.

Unusually Shaped

The female Asian sheepshead wrasse has thick lips and a forehead and chin that bulge out. They like to live in shallow, rocky environments. Some of them have been seen by shipwrecks.

Big Mouth

The female jawfish gives all her eggs to the male jawfish. He keeps them safe in his mouth until they hatch a week or two later.

Light On!

The deep-sea anglerfish has a built-in fishing rod that sticks out of its head. Bacteria glow at the tip, acting as a lure. Smaller fish are attracted to this light. When the small fish get close to the anglerfish's mouth, it's lights out!

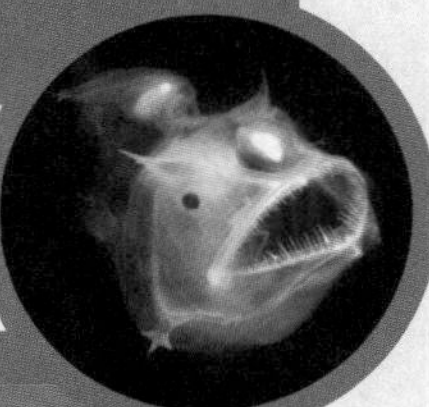

Groovy Fish

Have you ever heard of a frogfish? One species called *psychedelica* has wild stripes all over its body. This frogfish lives in Indonesia. It bounces along the ocean floor like a rubber ball!

Deadly Rock

The stonefish looks like, well, a stone. But don't be fooled, this rock can kill you. It's the world's most venomous fish. It is hard to spot, so watch your step!

Small Fry

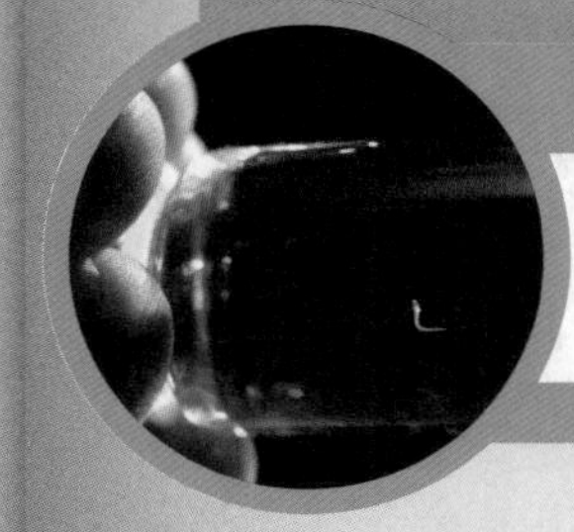

The world's smallest fish is the male stout infantfish. It is about 0.25 inches (0.63 centimeters) long. These fish have no teeth, scales, or color. They are very tough to spot!

Name: ______________________________ Date: ________________

Directions: Read "Fantastic Fish!" Then, answer the questions.

1. How could you change the suffix in the word *weirdest* to make a new word?

- Ⓐ replace *weird* with *tall*
- Ⓑ replace *–est* with *–er*
- Ⓒ replace *weird* with *–ing*
- Ⓓ replace *–est* with *–s*

2. Which fish is the world's most venomous?

- Ⓐ stonefish
- Ⓑ female Asian sheepshead wrasse
- Ⓒ male stout infantfish
- Ⓓ jawfish

3. What is the meaning of the word *tough* in the "Small Fry" section?

- Ⓐ chewy
- Ⓑ dangerous
- Ⓒ strong
- Ⓓ difficult

4. Which word is an antonym of *small*?

- Ⓐ ball
- Ⓑ large
- Ⓒ smaller
- Ⓓ tiny

5. What does *it's lights out* mean? Write a sentence using the phrase correctly.

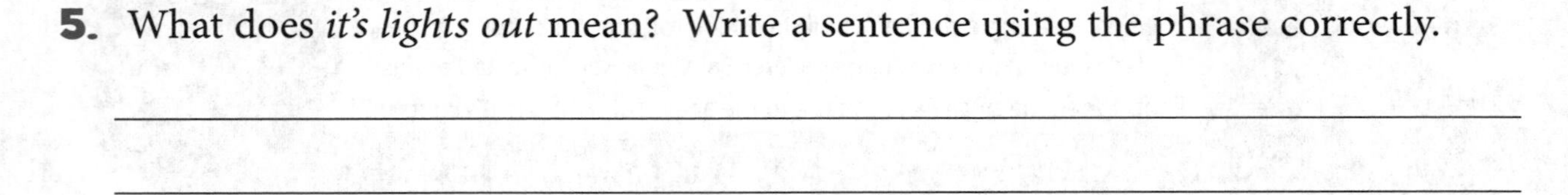

Name: ____________________ Date: ____________

Directions: Closely read these texts. Then, study the text on page 23. Look for content words that readers might need defined. Complete the chart with at least one word for each text.

Close-Reading Texts

Blue Whales: Ocean Giants	Making the Team
Blue whales eat tiny shrimp-like animals called krill. Blue whales don't have teeth like humans do. Instead, blue whales have baleen (bay-LEEN). When blue whales are hungry, they swallow a large amount of water. Then, they use their huge tongues to force the water out of their mouths. The baleen keeps the krill inside their mouths while the rest of the water is pushed out. Then, they can swallow their food.	Time seemed to slow down, and all Kyle focused on was his breathing and the sparkling water below. The coach blew his whistle and Kyle plunged in, churning through the water as quickly as he could. When he reached the other side of the pool, he popped up and grasped the steel ladder at the pool's edge, shaking his dripping hair out of his eyes. He climbed out of the water and returned to where the coach was standing.

Title	Content Word	Definition
Blue Whales: Ocean Giants		
Making the Team		
Fantastic Fish!		

Name: ______________________________ Date: ________________

Directions: Closely read these texts. Then, compare and contrast the two animals using the Venn diagram.

Close-Reading Texts

Sea Turtles: Ocean Reptiles	Manatees: Gentle Giants
Green sea turtles are reptiles, just like other turtles. They live in tropical coastal waters. Green sea turtles are very large. They have flippers for swimming and large, smooth carapaces (KEHR-uh-pay-sihs), or shells, that protect them. Green sea turtles sometimes migrate long distances to go from their feeding grounds to their nesting grounds. At their nesting grounds, they lay their eggs.	Manatees are large, gentle mammals that live underwater. They can grow up to 13 feet (4 meters) long. Manatees are related to elephants, but they do not have trunks. Manatees have flippers. They also have flat tails. Their flippers and tails help them move in the water. Boats are dangerous for manatees. Boats have underwater propellers with fast blades. These propellers can hurt or kill manatees.

Sea Turtles **Manatees**

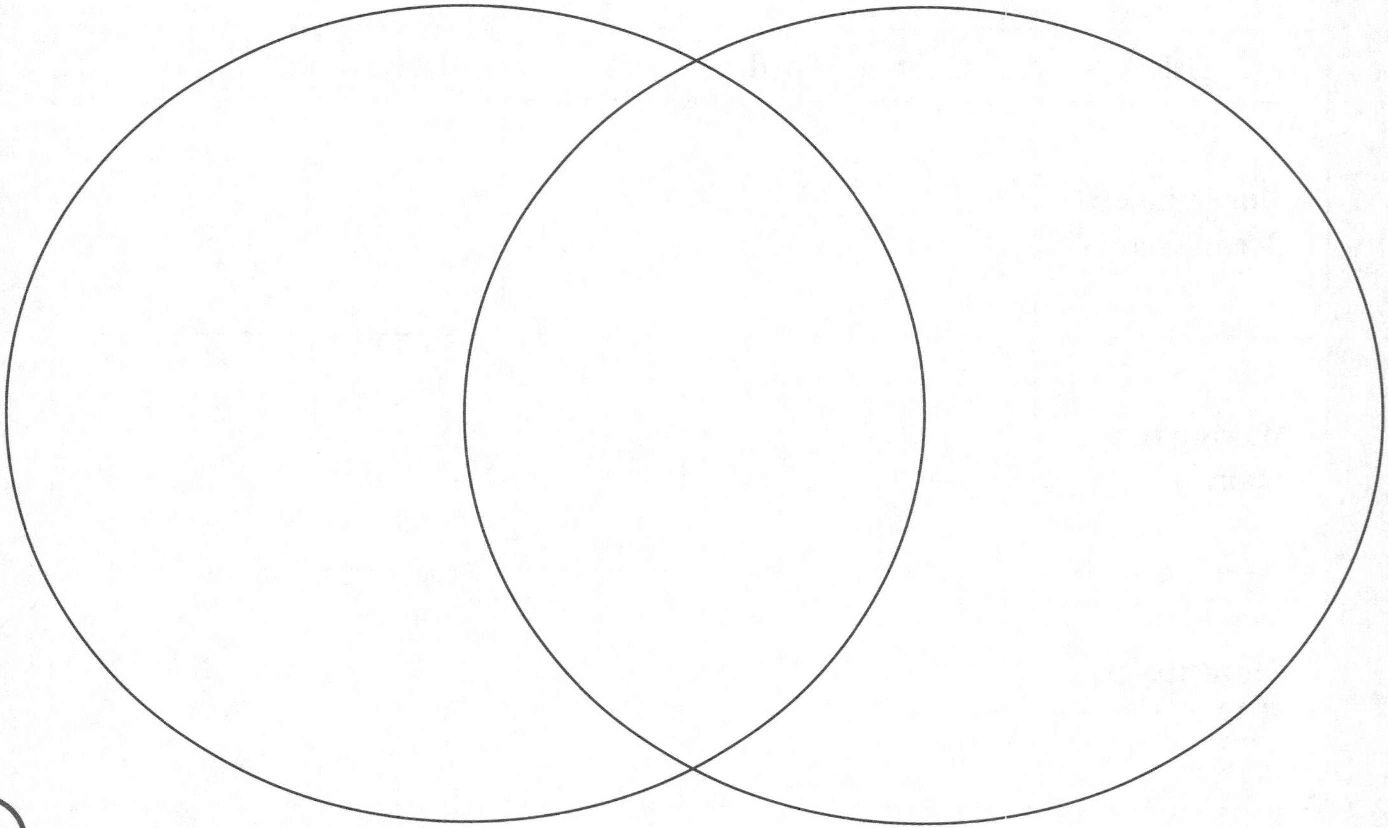

Name: ______________________________ Date: ________________

Directions: Think about the texts from this unit. Then, respond to the prompt.

Imagine you work for a magazine for people that snorkel or dive in the ocean. Write a short article informing readers about three animals you learned about in this unit.

Name: ______________________________ Date: ______________

Directions: Think of a topic you know at least four facts about. It might be a sport, hobby, animal, place, or something else. Write a fact sheet using your four pieces of information. Then, draw a picture to go along with your facts.

Title: ______________________________

Name: ____________________ Date: ____________

Directions: Read the text, and answer the questions.

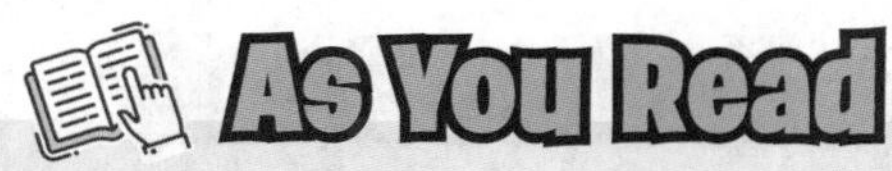

Circle unfamiliar words and underline any context clues for the words you circle.

Labrador Retrievers

Labrador retrievers are originally from Newfoundland. This is a part of Canada. Labrador retrievers are also called Labs. This breed of dog is popular around the world. And Labs are the most popular breed in the United States.

If you're looking for a family dog, a Labrador retriever might be the dog for you. Labs are great with children. They are very gentle. They enjoy being with their families. Labs also love to be active. They are smart and learn fast. Some people even train their Labs to be skilled hunting dogs. Labs come in three different colors: black, chocolate (brown), and yellow. Whichever color of Lab you choose, your Lab will be a friendly, loving pet!

1. Which sentence from the text best shares the main idea?
   - (A) Whichever color of Lab you choose, your Lab will be a friendly, loving pet!
   - (B) Labs are great with children.
   - (C) They also enjoy being with their families.
   - (D) Labrador retrievers are originally from Newfoundland.

2. What is the suffix in hunting?
   - (A) *–ing*
   - (B) hunt
   - (C) *suf–*
   - (D) hunting

3. What color is a chocolate Lab?
   - (A) black
   - (B) white
   - (C) spotted
   - (D) brown

4. What is the author's purpose?
   - (A) to entertain
   - (B) to persuade
   - (C) to inform
   - (D) to express

Name: ______________________ Date: ______________

Directions: Read the text, and answer the questions.

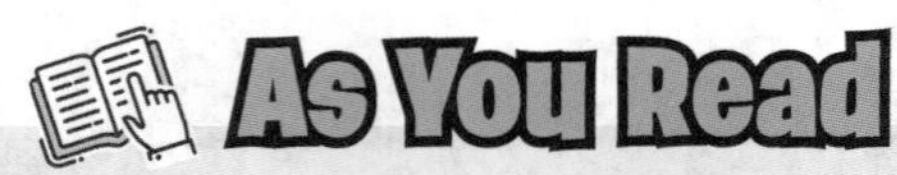

Circle unfamiliar words and underline any context clues.

Irish Wolfhounds

Have you ever wondered how tall dogs can get? Look no further than the Irish wolfhound. Irish wolfhounds are the tallest breed of dog. Their average height is between 31–33 inches (79–84 centimeters) tall. That's almost as tall as the average two-year-old human. When standing on their hind legs, Irish wolfhounds can stretch up to seven feet (two meters)! These dogs are quite big. So, they do best when they have large yards where they can play.

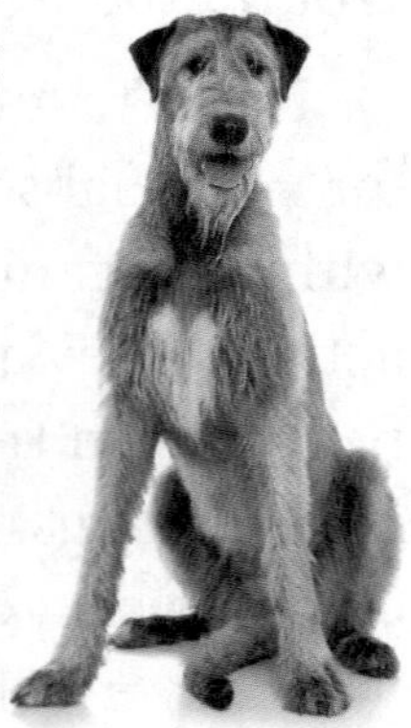

Irish wolfhounds are good with people. They are loyal to their families. They are friendly with strangers. Even though they are large, Irish wolfhounds are also very good with kids. They seem to know that they have to be careful around small children.

1. Which statement is **not** true?
   - (A) Irish wolfhounds are very big, tall dogs.
   - (B) Irish wolfhounds are loyal animals.
   - (C) Irish wolfhounds do not need a lot of space.
   - (D) Irish wolfhounds are good with young children.

2. What is the suffix in the word *careful*?
   - (A) *–ly*
   - (B) care–
   - (C) *–ful*
   - (D) full

3. Which definition of *hind* is used in the text?
   - (A) back or rear
   - (B) female deer
   - (C) nice
   - (D) front

4. Which best describes the tone?
   - (A) serious
   - (B) informative
   - (C) childish
   - (D) snobbish

Name: ______________________ Date: ______________

Directions: Read the text, and answer the questions.

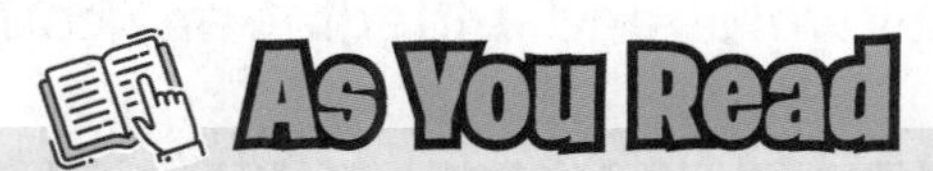

Circle unfamiliar words and underline any context clues.

Basenjis

If you think that all dogs bark, you haven't met the basenji (buh-SEHN-jee). Basenjis do not bark, but they still make noise. Basenjis can squeak, whine, and even yodel!

Basenjis were first bred in Africa. They were later brought to the United States in 1941. Basenjis have short, fine coats. They don't need a lot of grooming.

Training basenjis early is very important. They are very active, playful dogs. So, they need a lot of exercise and attention. They need to be trained to obey commands and walk on a leash. One great thing about basenjis is that they are intelligent and learn fast. This makes their training a lot easier.

1. What is a yodel?
   - (A) a breed of dog
   - (B) a small toy
   - (C) a kind of sound
   - (D) a bright color

2. Which word has the same root as *breed*?
   - (A) bread
   - (B) breathe
   - (C) bead
   - (D) breeding

3. What is something unusual about basenjis?

____

____

4. What type of person would be a good match for a basenji? Explain your answer.

____

____

Name: ______________________________ Date: ________________

Circle unfamiliar words and underline any context clues.

Which Dog Is Right for You?

"Yes, we can get a dog." These words can be very exciting to hear. But before you bring a dog home, there are some things you need to decide. One of those things is which breed of dog to choose. Here are some questions to help you choose the right dog for your lifestyle and personality.

How much space do you have?

Dogs come in many different sizes. First, make sure your home has enough space for your new family member. If you live in an apartment, a small breed, such as a pug or a Boston terrier, is a good option. If you live in a house with plenty of space, you may want a larger breed. Some very popular large breeds are Labrador retrievers and standard poodles.

Who is in your family?

Some dog breeds, such as the golden retriever, are very good with little children. Other breeds, such as the border collie, prefer older children. How many children are in your family? How old are they? Make sure the dog you choose is right for all the members of your family.

How active is your family?

All dogs need exercise, but some breeds of dogs are more active than others. Does your family like to go hiking or camping? Do you play sports? You may want an active breed. Some popular active breeds are the Irish setter and the Jack Russell terrier. If your family is less active, you may want a dog that requires less activity. Basset hounds and cocker spaniels are less active breeds.

How much time do you have?

Dogs need to be regularly trained, fed, walked, and groomed. Plus, you'll need to play with your dog. These things take a lot of time. Some breeds, such as the Pekingese, need to be groomed carefully every day. Other breeds, such as the short-legged dachshund, need a lot of training. Make sure you have time in your schedule to care for the dog you choose.

Name: ______________________________ Date: ______________

Directions: Read "Which Dog Is Right for You?" Then, answer the questions.

1. Based on the title, which prediction about the text is most accurate?

- (A) It is about how to correct the behavior of dogs that misbehave.
- (B) It is about selecting a dog that best suits one's lifestyle.
- (C) It is about dogs from the West Coast and the East Coast.
- (D) It is about a trip to the vet.

2. A reader would most likely read the text if he or she wanted to _____.

- (A) get a Basset hound.
- (B) make sure to choose the right breed of dog for themselves.
- (C) get a cat.
- (D) get the smallest dog they can find.

3. Which breed of dog might not be a good choice if you live in an apartment?

- (A) standard poodle
- (B) pug
- (C) Boston terrier
- (D) dachshund

4. What is the main idea of the first paragraph?

- (A) You won't have to make many decisions when you get a dog.
- (B) It is scary to get a new dog.
- (C) Different breeds of dogs are right for different people.
- (D) Everyone should get a new dog.

5. Make a web showing the important things to consider when getting a new dog.

Choosing the Right Dog

Name: ______________________________ Date: ______________

Directions: Reread "Which Dog Is Right for You?" Then, respond to the prompt.

Imagine your family is looking to adopt a dog from a local shelter. Write the shelter a letter describing your family. Write about the space you have in your home. Include how much time you can spend with the dog every day and what activity level you are looking for. Also, share what type of dog you think might be a good match for your family and why.

Name: ______________________ Date: ______________

Directions: Read the text, and answer the questions.

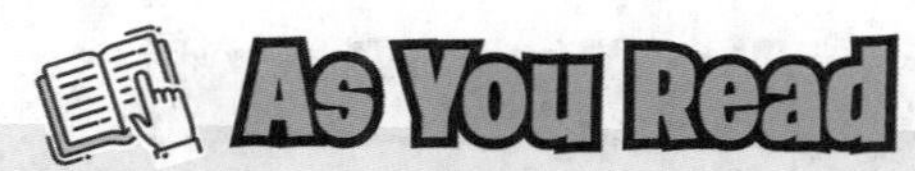

Number three important chronological events in the story.

A Dog's Life

It all started when Kim's best friend adopted a puppy.

"Barker is so cute!" said Kim. "Is it a pain to take care of her?"

"Not really," Keri said. "My big brother mostly takes care of her. My job is to play with her."

Kim was jealous. She wanted a dog. She began to notice dogs everywhere. They were on TV commercials, in internet videos doing adorable things, and in movies—sometimes even starring in them.

"Can I have a dog?" she finally asked her mother.

Her mom replied, "I don't think you're ready to raise a dog yet."

But Kim was determined, so she kept asking. Every day, her mother shook her head no. Kim kept pleading for a dog, telling her mother that Keri said it was easy to take care of a dog. And eventually, her mother gave in.

"I hope you're up for the responsibility," Kim's mom said.

"I am," Kim promised.

1. Which is a synonym for *jealous*?

- (A) envious
- (B) joyous
- (C) angry
- (D) confused

2. What does *a pain* mean in, *Is it a pain to take care of her?*

- (A) easy
- (B) injured
- (C) annoying
- (D) careful

3. Who takes care of Keri's dog?

- (A) Keri
- (B) Kim
- (C) Keri's brother
- (D) Kim's mom

4. Which event happens first?

- (A) Kim asks for a dog.
- (B) Kim sees dogs on TV.
- (C) Kim gets a dog.
- (D) Keri adopts a dog.

Name: ______________________________ Date: ______________

Directions: Read the text, and answer the questions.

Number three important chronological events in the story.

In the Shelter

Her mom drove to an animal shelter. Before they went inside, a volunteer explained that the shelter took in stray animals. They also housed animals that people had abandoned or given up.

Kim told the volunteer, "I want a cute little poodle or a pug that will fit in my backpack!"

The volunteer thought for a moment and said, "I don't think we have either of those breeds at the moment. We typically get mixed breeds, or mutts, at our shelter. They're the offspring of dogs of different breeds."

Kim was a little bummed to hear that, but she was certain she could find a dog she liked. She went inside with her mom, and they walked down the aisle, looking into cages. Some dogs were shy. Other dogs leaped up to greet her.

In one cage, a cute brown and white dog licked her hand through the bars. He wasn't a poodle or a pug, but he stole her heart.

"I want this one," she said. "I'll call him Duke."

1. What suffix is in the word *explained*?
   - (A) *–ed*
   - (B) *–ned*
   - (C) *–ex*
   - (D) *–d*

2. What is a *mutt*?
   - (A) a puppy
   - (B) a mixed-breed dog
   - (C) a brown and white dog
   - (D) an abandoned dog

3. Kim wants a pug because ______.
   - (A) it is the cutest breed
   - (B) Keri has one, too
   - (C) it will fit in her backpack
   - (D) it is abandoned

4. Which event happens last?
   - (A) Kim chooses a puppy.
   - (B) The volunteer shows Kim dogs.
   - (C) Kim goes to the shelter.
   - (D) Kim asks for a poodle or pug.

Name: ______________________________ Date: ______________

Directions: Read the text, and answer the questions.

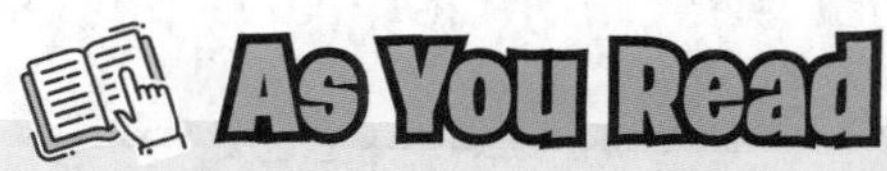

Number three important chronological events in the story.

Caring for Duke

At home, Kim immediately tried to teach Duke tricks. She wanted him to be able to high-five her. Her mom said, "Kim, we need to take care of him first."

Kim said, "You're right—I got carried away. The volunteer at the shelter said we should have him checked by a veterinarian. What does that mean?"

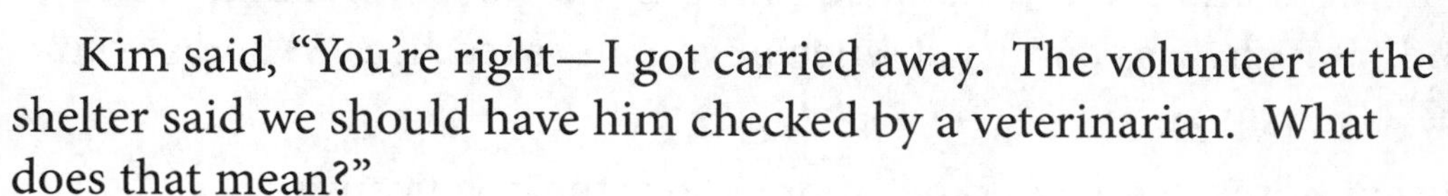

"A veterinarian checks animals to make sure they're healthy," her mom said.

Kim and her mom found a nearby vet's office. When they got there, the vet examined Duke and made sure he was up to date on all his shots. The vet also told Kim to bring Duke in for a rabies shot every year.

"Wow," said Kim. "I thought animals only went to the vet if they were sick."

Next, Kim and her mom went to the pet store to buy dog food. Kim purchased one brand, but Duke refused to eat it. They had to go back for another option—and then another! Finally, Duke liked one of the kinds of food! "Who knew that taking care of a dog was so much work?" Kim thought.

1. Which word is an antonym of *sick*?

- (A) smart
- (B) healthy
- (C) ill
- (D) bored

2. What does Kim want to do first?

- (A) take Duke to the vet
- (B) buy Duke food
- (C) walk Duke
- (D) teach Duke tricks

3. Why does Kim buy different types of dog food?

____

4. Is Kim being a good pet owner? Explain your reasoning.

____

____

Name: ______________________________ Date: ________________

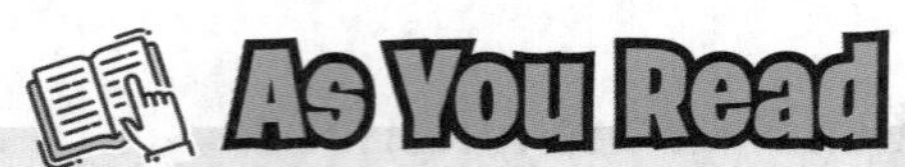

Number six important chronological events in the story.

Loving Her Dog Duke

Kim was petting Duke when her mom said, "Please walk Duke at least twice a day. He needs to exercise and go to the bathroom—outside!"

Kim rode her bike to the pet store and bought a leash and harness. When she got back, she tried the harness on Duke, but it was a little loose.

She took him out and proudly paraded him past the people walking in her neighborhood. But she was confused when a woman asked her, "Where's your dog's license?"

When she got home, Kim asked her mom about the dog license.

"I wish you had done more to prepare for owning a dog," her mother said. "Yes, we'll need to apply for a dog license."

Kim sighed as she worked with her mom on applying for the license. *What next?* she thought to herself. She got her answer days later.

Before taking Duke out for a walk, Kim tied his leash to the back door and went inside to get some garbage bags. But when Kim returned, Duke had slipped out of his too-loose harness and was nowhere in sight.

Kim felt awful. She ran outside in a panic and jogged down the street.

"Have you seen a little dog?" she asked desperately to everyone she passed. Then, she returned home and told her mom Duke had run away.

"Let's not panic," her mom said calmly. "Let's think of how we can find him."

Kim thought for a moment, and then, without a word, ran upstairs to her computer and began creating a missing dog flyer. Kim and her mom posted them everywhere in their neighborhood while keeping an eye out for Duke.

The doorbell rang in the morning. Kim sprinted to the front door and swung it open to see a woman standing there with Duke!

"I found this adorable dog in my backyard," the woman said, smiling. "I believe he belongs to you."

Kim was ecstatic and so relieved, but she also felt guilty for losing Duke.

"I'm so sorry, Duke," Kim told him, rubbing his chin. "I'll get you a new harness now—I always have to put your needs ahead of my needs."

Duke wagged his tail and barked. He loved Kim no matter what!

Name: ______________________________ Date: ________________

Directions: Read "Loving Her Dog Duke." Then, answer the questions.

1. Which word has the same prefix as *researched*?
   - (A) asked
   - (B) parched
   - (C) redwood
   - (D) review

2. Which word is a synonym for *ecstatic*?
   - (A) disappointed
   - (B) funny
   - (C) busy
   - (D) excited

3. Which word does **not** describe how Kim feels when Duke is missing?
   - (A) sad
   - (B) guilty
   - (C) relieved
   - (D) worried

4. What does Kim do to try and find Duke?
   - (A) She makes missing dog posters.
   - (B) She calls all of her neighbors.
   - (C) She asks her friends to help her find him.
   - (D) She talks to the vet.

5. Describe four events from the story in chronological order.

1.	
2.	
3.	
4.	

Name: ______________________________ Date: ______________

Directions: Reread "Loving Her Dog Duke." Then, respond to the prompt.

This story was told from Kim's point of view. Think about the important events in the story. Then, rewrite the story describing those events from Duke's point of view!

Name: ________________________ Date: ____________

Conversation with My Dog

I wish I could talk with my little brown pooch.

If we could converse, I'd give her a smooch.

I tell her to sit and go fetch a ball,

and those commands she does recall.

But when I ask her how she feels,

no matter how many times I appeal,

she just looks into my eyes

and never, never, ever replies,

not even with a bark.

She knows when I'm sad

and when I'm plenty mad.

I can read her feelings on her face.

Her emotions there are easy to trace.

But when I tell my dog I love her a lot,

I wish she'd be able to readily exclaim

that she feels about me exactly the same!

Name: ______________________________ Date: ______________

Directions: Read "Conversation with My Dog." Then, answer the questions.

1. Which word does **not** rhyme with *eyes*?
   - (A) tries
   - (B) wise
   - (C) twice
   - (D) dies

2. What type of text is this?
   - (A) poem
   - (B) story
   - (C) play
   - (D) song

3. What does the boy want in this text?
   - (A) for his dog to talk to him
   - (B) to talk to his dog
   - (C) for his dog to play fetch
   - (D) to teach his dog commands

4. What is a *smooch*?
   - (A) treat
   - (B) praise
   - (C) game
   - (D) kiss

5. How does the boy feel about his dog? Support your answer using the text.

____

____

____

____

____

____

Name: ______________________________ Date: ________________

Directions: Closely read these texts. Then, finish the web to show different responsibilities of being a pet owner.

Close-Reading Texts

Which Dog Is Right for You?	Caring for Duke
Dogs need to be regularly trained, fed, walked, and groomed. Plus, you'll need to play with your dog. These things take a lot of time. Some breeds, such as the Pekingese, need to be groomed carefully every day. Other breeds, such as the short-legged dachshund, need a lot of training. Make sure you have time in your schedule to care for the dog you choose.	At home, Kim immediately tried to teach Duke tricks. She wanted him to be able to high-five her. Her mom said, "Kim, we need to take care of him first." Kim said, "You're right—I got carried away. The volunteer at the shelter said we should have him checked by a veterinarian. What does that mean?" "A veterinarian checks animals to make sure they're healthy," her mom said. Kim and her mom found a nearby vet's office.

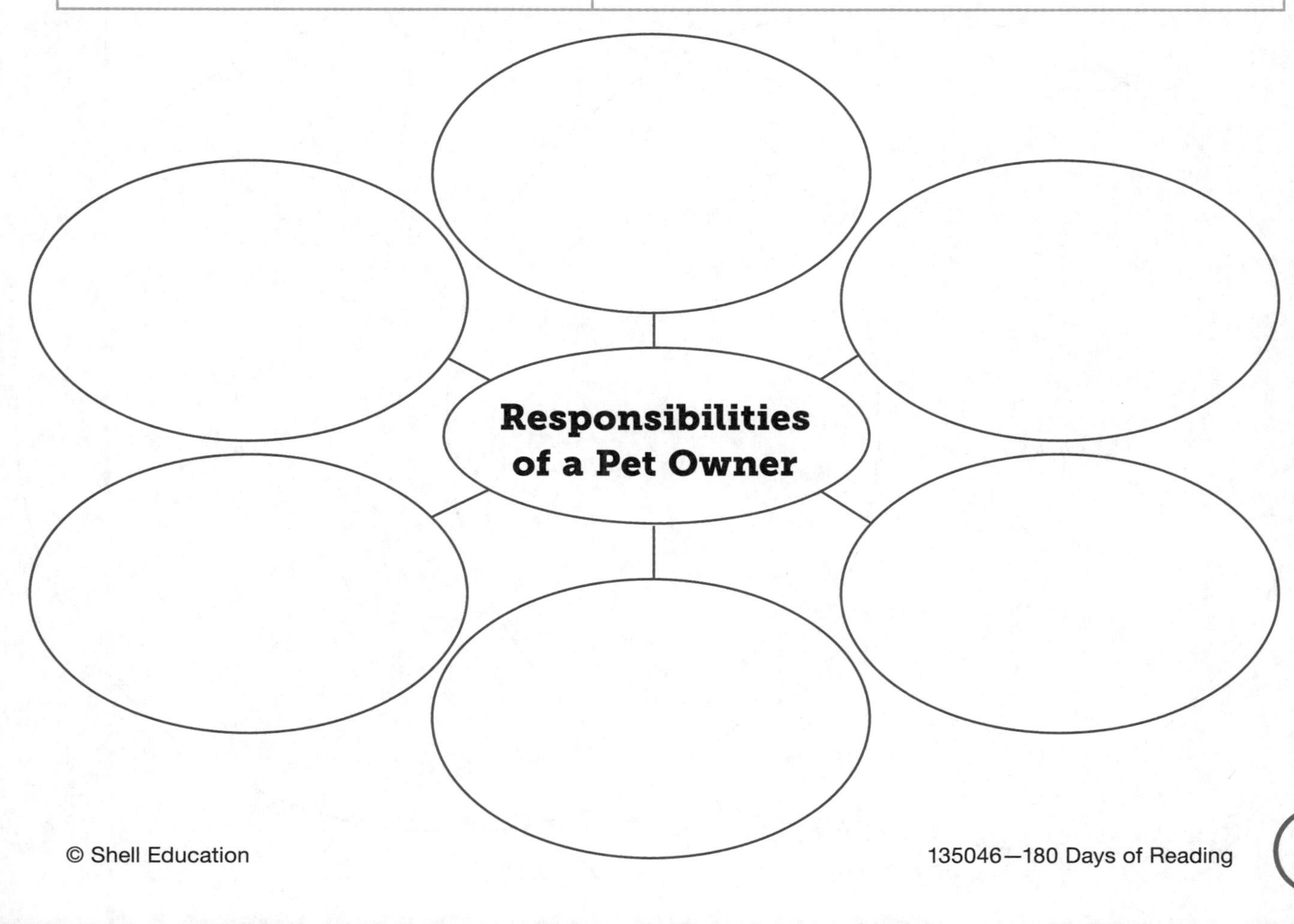

Name: ______________________________ Date: ________________

Directions: Closely read these texts. Then, compare and contrast the two texts using the Venn diagram.

Close-Reading Texts

Basenjis	Conversation with My Dog
Training basenjis early is very important. They are very active, playful dogs. So, they need a lot of exercise and attention. They need to be trained to obey commands and walk on a leash. One great thing about basenjis is that they are intelligent and learn fast. This makes their training a lot easier.	I tell her to sit and go fetch a ball, and those commands she does recall. But when I ask her how she feels, no matter how many times I appeal, she just looks into my eyes and never, never, ever replies, not even with a bark.

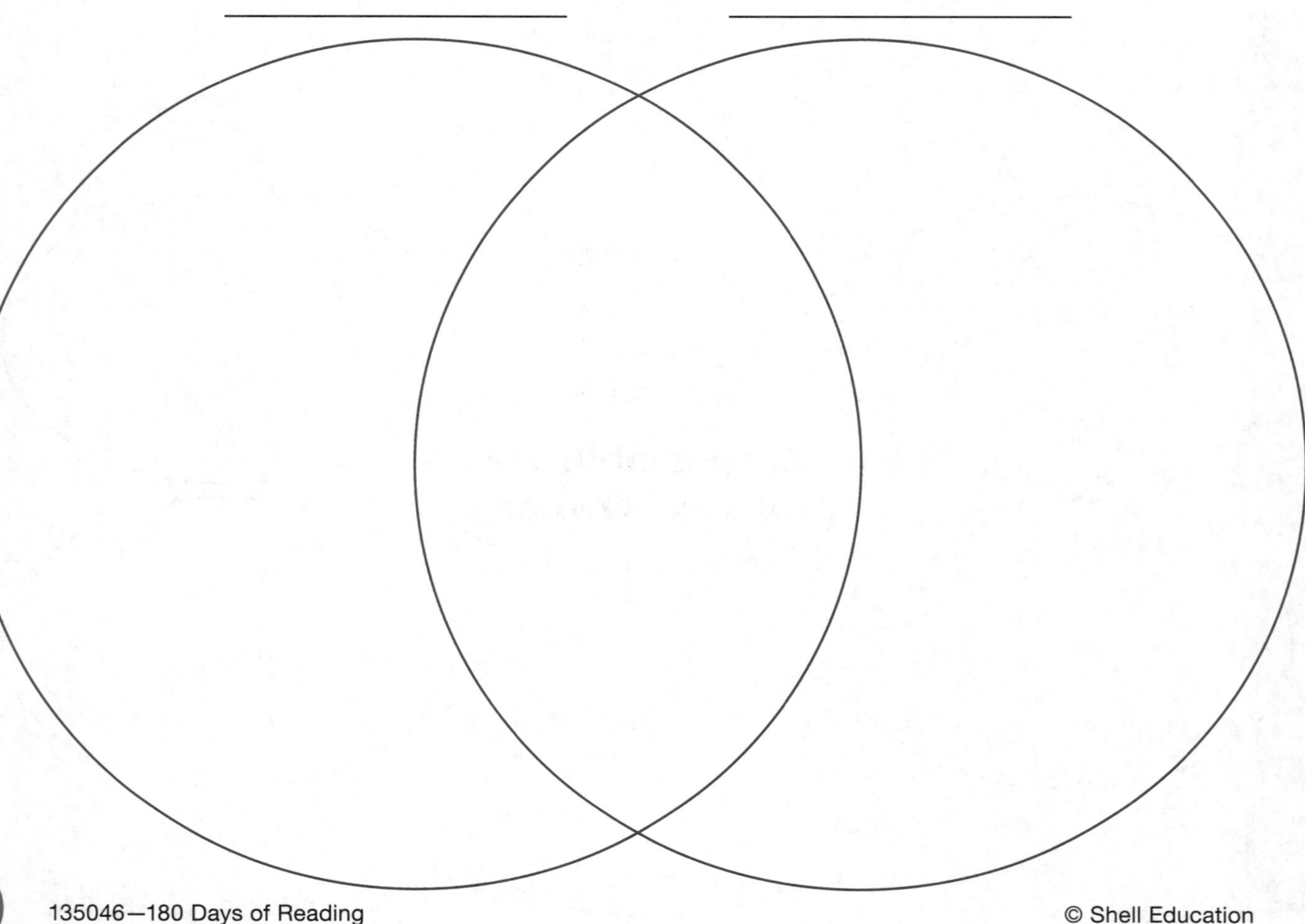

Name: ______________________ Date: ____________

Directions: Reread "Conversation with My Dog." Then, respond to the prompt.

What if the boy's dog could talk for just one day? What would they talk about and ask each other? Write a short story about the day the boy and his dog can have a conversation.

Name: ______________________________ Date: ______________

Directions: Write a poem about an animal. The poem should be at least eight lines and follow the same rhyme pattern as "Conversation with My Dog."

Name: ______________________________ Date: ______________

Directions: Read the text, and answer the questions.

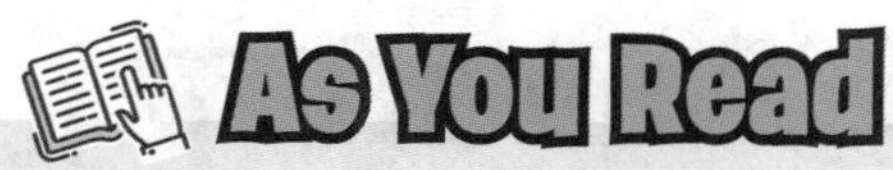

Add a checkmark next to any information you have learned before.

Safety Tips

Fire safety is important. This is because fires can be dangerous. Here are some things you can do to keep your home safe.

- Always cook with an adult.
- Do not play in the kitchen.
- Be careful around stoves, fireplaces, and heaters. Keep towels and flammables (FLAH-muh-buhlz) away from them.
- Do not place clothes or other flammables on lamps.
- Do not plug too many items into an electrical outlet.
- Do not play with matches or lighters.

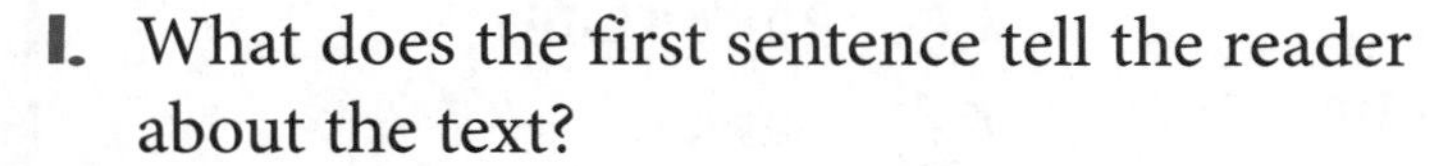

1. What does the first sentence tell the reader about the text?
   - Ⓐ This is about the best ways to start fires.
   - Ⓑ This is about how to heat things without using fire.
   - Ⓒ This is about tragedies that occurred because of fires.
   - Ⓓ This is about how to be safe when around fires.

2. What is the main idea?
   - Ⓐ Adults should do the cooking.
   - Ⓑ Do not play with matches or lighters.
   - Ⓒ There are things you can do to be safe and prevent fires.
   - Ⓓ Fires are very dangerous.

3. The word *flammables* has ______.
   - Ⓐ one syllable
   - Ⓑ two syllables
   - Ⓒ three syllables
   - Ⓓ four syllables

4. What is an antonym of *always*?
   - Ⓐ never
   - Ⓑ don't
   - Ⓒ away
   - Ⓓ from

Name: ______________________________ Date: ________________

Directions: Read the text, and answer the questions.

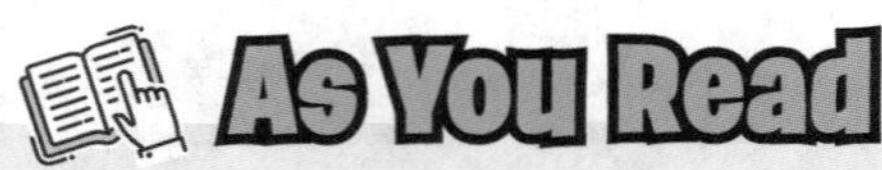

Add a checkmark next to any information you have learned before.

Smoke Alarms

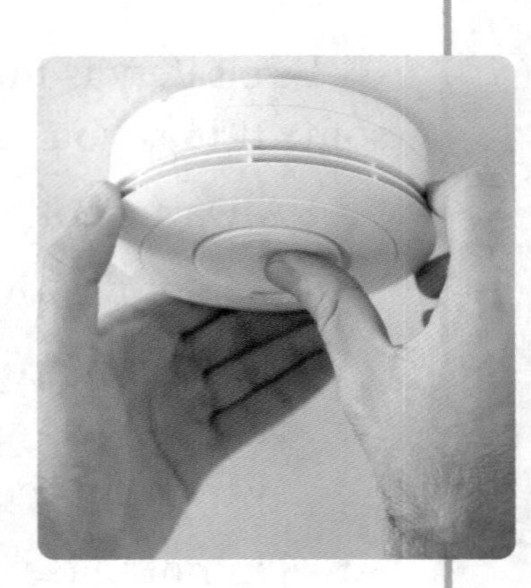

Taking good care of the smoke alarms in a home is important. Smoke alarms warn people when there is a fire. This allows people the time to call the fire department. People can help smoke alarms do their jobs. Every month, they can test the smoke alarms. Testing them helps people know if they are working properly. It is also important to change the batteries in smoke alarms. The batteries should be changed every year. Checking the alarms and changing the batteries takes just a few minutes. But these small checks make a big difference in fire safety!

1. Which statement is **not** based on information from the text?
   - (A) Change the batteries in your smoke alarm every five years.
   - (B) Changing the batteries in smoke alarms is important.
   - (C) People can check that smoke alarms are working.
   - (D) Changing the batteries takes a few minutes.

2. Which word part in *properly* is the suffix?
   - (A) *–ly*
   - (B) proper
   - (C) *prop–*
   - (D) *pro–*

3. A synonym for *properly* is _____.
   - (A) important
   - (B) safety
   - (C) should
   - (D) correctly

4. Which word best describes the tone?
   - (A) frightened
   - (B) comical
   - (C) serious
   - (D) informal

Name: ______________________________ Date: ______________

Directions: Read the text, and answer the questions.

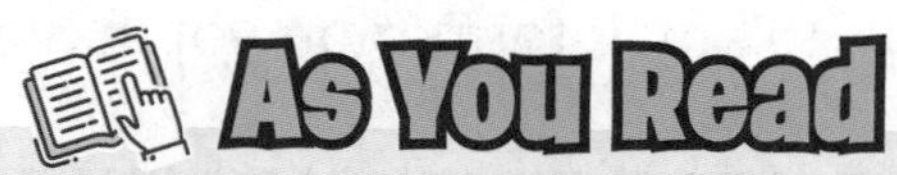

Add a checkmark next to any information you have learned before.

How Fires Start

All fires need three things to burn: oxygen, fuel, and a heat source. Just about anything that can burn can be fuel. But some items, such as wood and cloth, burn more easily than others. Items that burn easily should be stored carefully to reduce the chances of a fire starting. Fires also need a source of heat. Lamps, matches, lighters, and stoves are all sources of heat. So if you keep heat sources away from things that burn easily, you can prevent fires from starting.

1. Which is **not** a source of heat?
   - (A) stoves
   - (B) matches
   - (C) oxygen
   - (D) lamps

2. In which point of view is the text written?
   - (A) first person
   - (B) second person
   - (C) third person
   - (D) none of the above

3. What three things are needed for a fire to start?

____

____

____

4. What are two specific things you can do to prevent a fire in your home?

____

____

____

____

Name: ________________________________ Date: ________________

Add a checkmark next to any information you have learned before.

The Work of a Firefighter

Do you know what firefighters do? They put out fires and save people. They visit schools to talk about fire safety. They do a lot of other things, too.

Firefighters go through lots of training and practice to do their jobs. First, they learn about fire science. This helps them understand how fires act and spread. They also learn new ways to put out fires. They are taught how to use specialized tools. Finally, they learn how to act as a team. It is not easy to put out fires, and firefighters have to work together quickly. Everyone on a firefighting team has to know exactly what to do. This can take a lot of practice! So, firefighters practice together to get ready for a real fire.

Firefighters do their best work when they are prepared. They stay fit and healthy. They exercise so they can keep up with the demands of the job. Firefighters also take good care of their gear and their tools. They stay organized so they don't have to rush when they're called to a job. They clean their trucks and fix any issues they're having. This way, when there is a fire, all their gear works properly.

Firefighters help people in a variety of situations. When people get hurt, firefighters often get to the scene first. Firefighters know how to give first aid. As part of their training, they are taught how to give special kinds of first aid. Firefighters help people when they are not fighting fires, too. Some firefighters teach people about fire safety. They teach people how to prevent fires and what to do if there is a fire. Some firefighters visit schools. Other firefighters talk about fire safety on the radio and TV.

Fires are dangerous and can be scary for most people. But firefighters are there to help keep people safe.

Name: ______________________ Date: ______________

Directions: Read "The Work of a Firefighter." Then, answer the questions.

1. A reader would most likely read the text to _____.
   - (A) learn more about how to put out fires
   - (B) be informed about fire safety
   - (C) be entertained by a fictional story about fire
   - (D) learn more about firefighters

2. Which alternative title does **not** fit the text?
   - (A) A Firefighter's Job
   - (B) What Firefighters Do
   - (C) How to Drive a Firetruck
   - (D) Firefighters: At Work

3. Knowing about _____ would help the reader understand the text.
   - (A) first aid
   - (B) teamwork
   - (C) fire
   - (D) all of the above

4. When do firefighters do their jobs best?
   - (A) when they are in good shape
   - (B) when they are sleepy
   - (C) when they are loud
   - (D) when they are dirty

5. Make a list of five things firefighters do so they are ready for their job.

   1. ______________________________
   2. ______________________________
   3. ______________________________
   4. ______________________________
   5. ______________________________

Name: ______________________________ Date: ______________

Directions: Reread "The Work of a Firefighter." Then, respond to the prompt.

Write a paragraph explaining why you would or would not like to be a firefighter. Support your reasoning using at least three details from the text. Don't forget an introduction and a conclusion sentence.

Name: ______________________________ Date: ________________

Directions: Read the text, and answer the questions.

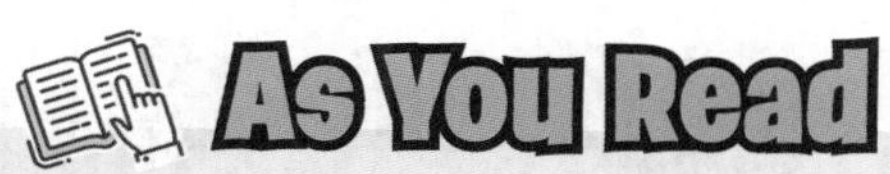

Make a note about one connection you see between the text and yourself.

Fear of Fire

Willa didn't think much about fires. Her house had a nice fireplace, and there was a gas flame on the kitchen stove when it was on, but it was not very scary. Sometimes, when she watched the news on TV, she saw stories about blazing fires destroying buildings. They were terrible, but they didn't have anything to do with her.

But then one day, one of her classmates didn't show up for school.

Her teacher said, "There was a fire at Shawn's house last night. No one was hurt, but his house burned down, and his family has to find a new place to live."

Willa was shocked. She felt bad for Shawn and wondered how it had happened. She started to wonder if it could happen to her home. But she shrugged that away, and she asked her teacher how they could help Shawn.

After that day, the danger of fire became real to Willa. She started to pay attention to stories about fires. She learned that many of them occurred because people didn't think about fire safety. Willa was determined to not make that mistake.

1. Which word is a compound word?

- (A) mistake
- (B) fireplace
- (C) attention
- (D) danger

2. Which phrase shows you Willa is not concerned about fire?

- (A) ...they didn't have anything to do with her.
- (B) She felt bad for Shawn...
- (C) She started to pay attention...
- (D) She saw stories about blazing fires destroying buildings.

3. Which word is a synonym for *worried*?

- (A) confident
- (B) calm
- (C) angry
- (D) concerned

4. How many syllables is the word *destroying*?

- (A) one syllable
- (B) two syllables
- (C) three syllables
- (D) four syllables

Name: ______________________ Date: ______________

Directions: Read the text, and answer the questions.

Make a note about one connection you see between the text and yourself.

Finding Fire Hazards

Willa learned everything she could about fire prevention. One afternoon, she was at her friend Tess's house. Tess went to light a candle on the dining room table, and Willa gasped.

"Be careful!" Willa yelled. "That tablecloth looks flammable."

Tess scoffed at her and said, "Relax. I know how to use a match."

The next day, Willa saw a kid in the park burning leaves using a magnifying lens. She ran over and told him, "Stop! Those burning leaves could start a fire."

At home, Willa pointed out fire hazards to her brother, Ronnie. She reminded him to not put his winter beanie over his lamp because it could catch fire.

She even criticized her parents.

"Dad, did you remember to get new batteries for the smoke alarm?" she asked.

Her family started to think that Willa was getting carried away with her fears.

1. Which suffix does **not** fit with the word *fool*?
   - (A) *–ish*
   - (B) *–er*
   - (C) *–s*
   - (D) *–ed*

2. What is the setting when Willa talks to Tess?
   - (A) bedroom
   - (B) dining room
   - (C) bathroom
   - (D) basement

3. What does the phrase *carried away* mean in the text?
   - (A) Willa's fears are taking her to another place.
   - (B) Willa is thinking about her fears too much.
   - (C) Willa is ignoring her fears.
   - (D) Willa's fears are not a big deal.

4. What is the kid using to burn leaves?
   - (A) magnifying glass
   - (B) battery
   - (C) match
   - (D) lighter

Name: ______________________________ Date: ______________

Directions: Read the text, and answer the questions.

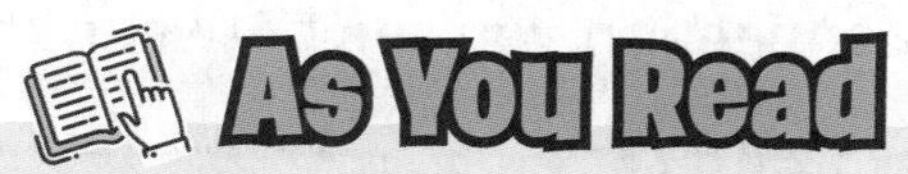

Make a note about one connection you see between the text and yourself.

Fire Drill

At school, an alarm roared loudly over and over.

"Alright, everyone, this is a fire drill," Willa's teacher said. Willa breathed a sigh of relief. She quickly left her chair, following her classmates out of their room. They walked outside to the far end of the playground. They stood in lines while the teachers took attendance and counted everyone.

After the drill ended, Willa thought about what would happen if a real fire started at school. Then, she wondered what would happen if a fire started at home. She realized her family was completely unprepared!

But when she mentioned this to her dad, he said, "Don't worry, there isn't much of a chance we'll have a fire. If we do, we'll just quickly leave the house."

Willa thought that his plan sounded like no plan at all.

She began to research fire evacuation plans. At school the next day, she told Tess about her fire plan and how everyone should come up with one.

"What are the chances my home will catch fire?" Tess asked. "You're getting carried away."

1. Which word is a synonym for *evacuation*?
   - (A) removal
   - (B) investigate
   - (C) gather
   - (D) safety

2. How would you describe Willa's dad's reaction to her fire plan suggestion?
   - (A) interested
   - (B) concerned
   - (C) dismissive
   - (D) angry

3. Why does Willa begin thinking about a fire plan for her home?

   ____

4. Describe two ideas Willa might use for her home's fire plan.

   ____

   ____

Name: ______________________________ Date: ______________

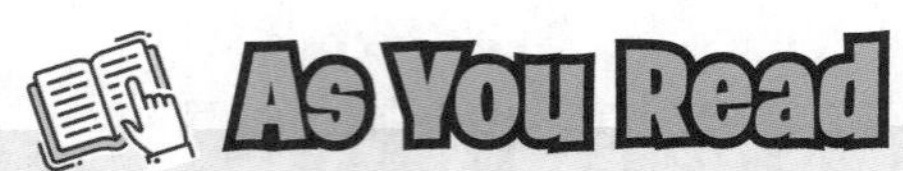

Make a note about one connection you see between the text and yourself.

House on Fire

It was up to Willa to make her house safe from fire. She started by checking smoke alarms. She told her dad that each bedroom needed an alarm.

"That's not necessary," he said. "One alarm will wake everyone."

Willa showed him her research, and she got her way. Then, she started planning an escape from the house in case a fire happened. She even drew a map of escape routes and handed copies to her family.

A few months later, Willa was asleep when a loud screeching sound woke her. It was the smoke alarm! She smelled smoke coming from downstairs. Willa jumped out of bed and thought to herself, *don't panic—just follow the plan.*

The noise of the smoke alarms sent her dazed family into the hallway.

"There's a fire downstairs!" said Willa. "Remember the plan: we escape down the main stairway."

"We can't," said her mom, fearfully. "There's too much smoke!"

Right away, Willa said, "We'll use the backup emergency plan."

They all turned and went down the back stairway to the kitchen. Her dad reached out to the kitchen door and briefly touched the knob to feel for heat, just as Willa had instructed.

"It's hot," Willa's dad said. "The fire might be on the other side."

Ronnie cried, "Now what do we do?" It was getting hot now, and the smoke stung everyone's eyes.

Willa thought of her map and shouted, "The bathroom is our way out!"

Everyone crowded into the bathroom and her dad started to help everyone go through the window.

They gathered in the front yard while her mom called the fire department. After the blaze was put out, a firefighter told them the fire probably started in the wall of the kitchen. It wasn't their fault—it was bad electrical wiring. Their house was badly damaged, but most importantly, no one was hurt.

Ronnie said to Willa, "I just became a huge fan of your fire plan!"

Name: ________________________________ Date: ________________

Directions: Read "House on Fire." Then, answer the questions.

1. What is the suffix in the word *insisted*?
   (A) *–ted*
   (B) *–in*
   (C) *–ed*
   (D) *–sis*

2. How does Willa feel during the fire?
   (A) excited
   (B) bored
   (C) amused
   (D) calm

3. Which word is an antonym of *dazed*?
   (A) confused
   (B) aware
   (C) lost
   (D) injured

4. How does the family get out of their house during the fire?
   (A) the front door
   (B) the bathroom window
   (C) the back door
   (D) the attic

5. Choose two characters from the story. Write one way you and each character are the same and one way you are each different.

	Character	Same	Different
1.			
2.			

Name: ______________________ Date: ______________

Directions: Reread "House on Fire." Then, respond to the prompt.

Does your family have a fire plan? Write two different ways your family could exit your home in case of a fire. Draw a map for each one to show the route.

Plan 1

Plan	Map
________________ ________________ ________________ ________________ ________________ ________________ ________________ ________________	

Plan 2

Plan	Map
________________ ________________ ________________ ________________ ________________ ________________ ________________ ________________	

SENSATIONAL SMOKE JUMPERS

Smoke jumpers are special firefighters who jump from airplanes. They land near big fires in wild places, and they reach places that normal firefighters can't reach. A jumper's job is hard, and it can be dangerous. Here is a day in the life of these brave men and women.

1. A horn sounds, and a team of smoke jumpers spring into action. First, they put on special protective gear, including fire-resistant pants and shirts. Over that goes a strong material called Kevlar®. Helmets complete their outfits, and they're ready to go!

2. An airplane flies the smoke jumpers to a fire. They parachute down near the blaze. Then, the plane drops heavy boxes that contain tools to cut down trees. The airplane drops food and water for them, too.

3. On the ground, the jumpers don't use water to extinguish fires. Instead, they cut a fire line or fire break. They cut down trees and bushes. Sometimes, they dig trenches in the path of the fire. Without trees as a source of fuel, the fire will slow down or halt.

4. After the jumpers contain the fire, they cool down the area. Even if there's no smoke, there may be burning embers. So, the jumpers must stir the ashes. They cover the ashes with cool soil, which lowers the heat. Only then do the smoke jumpers pack up. They hike to a location where a truck can pick them up, and they return home.

Name: ______________________________ Date: ________________

Directions: Read "Sensational Smoke Jumpers." Then, answer the questions.

1. Which of these suffixes can be added to the word *spring*?

- (A) *–ful*
- (B) *–ly*
- (C) *–ed*
- (D) *–ing*

2. What is the past tense of the word *stir*?

- (A) stirred
- (B) stirring
- (C) starred
- (D) store

3. Which of these events happens last?

- (A) Jumpers cover ash with cool soil.
- (B) Jumpers put on protective gear.
- (C) Jumpers cut a fire line.
- (D) Tools are dropped for the jumpers.

4. What is the purpose of this text?

- (A) to persuade
- (B) to entertain
- (C) to scare
- (D) to inform

5. How do smoke jumpers contain fires?

____

____

____

____

Name: ______________________________ Date: ________________

Directions: Closely read these texts. Then, study the magazine page on page 59. Look for words or phrases describing fire safety. Then, write the words on the chart.

Close-Reading Texts

Smoke Alarms	Finding Fire Hazards
Smoke alarms warn people when there is a fire. This allows people the time to call the fire department. People can help smoke alarms do their jobs. Every month, they can test the smoke alarms. Testing them helps people know if they are working properly. It is also important to change the batteries in smoke alarms.	The next day, Willa saw a kid in the park burning leaves using a magnifying lens. She ran over and told him, "Stop! Those burning leaves could start a fire." At home, Willa pointed out fire hazards to her brother, Ronnie. She reminded him to not put his winter beanie over his lamp because it could catch fire. She even criticized her parents. "Dad, did you remember to get new batteries for the smoke alarm?"

Smoke Alarms	
Finding Fire Hazards	
Sensational Smoke Jumpers	

Name: ______________________ Date: ______________

Directions: Carefully read these texts. Then, compare the texts in the chart.

Close-Reading Texts

How Fires Start	House on Fire
All fires need three things to burn: oxygen, fuel, and a heat source. Just about anything that can burn can be fuel. But some items, such as wood and cloth, burn more easily than others. Items that burn easily should be stored carefully to reduce the chances of a fire starting. Fires also need a source of heat. Lamps, matches, lighters, and stoves are all sources of heat.	Right away, Willa said, "We'll use the backup emergency plan." They all turned and went down the back stairway to the kitchen. Her dad reached out to the kitchen door and briefly touched the knob to feel for heat, just as Willa had instructed. "It's hot," Willa's dad said. "The fire might be on the other side." Ronnie cried, "Now what do we do?" It was getting hot now, and the smoke stung everyone's eyes. Willa thought of her map and shouted, "The bathroom is our way out!" Everyone crowded into the bathroom and her dad started to help everyone go through the window.

	Purpose	Genre
How Fires Start		
House on Fire		
Both		

Name: ________________________________ Date: ______________

Directions: Reread "Sensational Smoke Jumpers." Then, respond to the prompt.

Imagine people in Willa's city found out about her dedication to fire safety. They are going to give her an award. The mayor is going to give a speech. She wants you to write it. The speech should tell Willa's history in fire safety and her actions on the night of the fire at her house.

Name: ________________________________ Date: ______________

Directions: Think of something you know how to do. It might be related to sports, hobbies, activities, or something else. Write a magazine article with captions and drawings like "Sensational Smoke Jumpers." Show how to accomplish your task.

Name: ______________________________ Date: ______________

Directions: Read the text, and answer the questions.

Put parentheses around words you think are important vocabulary in the text.

An Exciting City

Were you thinking of visiting a beautiful city? You might want to go to Rio de Janeiro. It is a large city in Brazil. Rio is on the coast. The city is known for having beautiful beaches. People can go swimming or diving. The beaches are popular with tourists. A popular time of the year to visit Rio is during Carnival. Carnival is a religious holiday. During this time, there are big parades. People dress in fancy costumes. There is a lot of music at Carnival. People around the world celebrate Carnival, too. But Rio's celebration is the largest in the world. Lastly, soccer is popular year-round in Rio. The city has four soccer teams! You could watch a game any day of the week. With its beaches, Carnival, and sports, there's always something to do in Rio.

1. In which chapter of a book would you expect to find this information?
   - (A) Chapter 1: Playing Soccer
   - (B) Chapter 2: Famous Carnivals of Canada
   - (C) Chapter 6: The Rio Grande
   - (D) Chapter 9: Visiting Rio de Janeiro

2. What is the root word in *tourist*?
   - (A) ist
   - (B) our
   - (C) tour
   - (D) uri

3. Which word is the antonym of *fancy*?
   - (A) plain
   - (B) dressy
   - (C) elegant
   - (D) purple

4. Which of the following is **not** part of Carnival?
   - (A) big parades
   - (B) music
   - (C) diving
   - (D) costumes

Name: ______________________ Date: ______________

Directions: Read the text, and answer the questions.

Put parentheses around words you think are important vocabulary in the text.

An Important Rain Forest

The Amazon Rain Forest is a special place. It is a tropical rain forest. That means it gets very warm. It also gets a lot of rain. It gets over 59 inches (150 centimeters) of rain per year! This is a lot more than most places on Earth. Also, the Amazon is home to one-half of the world's species. Many unique plants and animals live there. The rain forest provides many resources for them. These resources include water, trees, and oxygen. Many people work to protect life in this special place.

1. Which words could help a reader predict what this text is about?
   - (A) rain forest and species
   - (B) temperatures and river
   - (C) Atlantic and protect
   - (D) animals and special

2. Which best describes the climate of the Amazon Rain Forest?
   - (A) dry and cold
   - (B) wet and cold
   - (C) dry and hot
   - (D) wet and hot

3. Which word is **not** plural?
   - (A) temperatures
   - (B) means
   - (C) inches
   - (D) animals

4. What does the word *species* mean?
   - (A) stories
   - (B) zoos
   - (C) types
   - (D) fish

Name: ______________________________ Date: ______________

Directions: Read the text, and answer the questions.

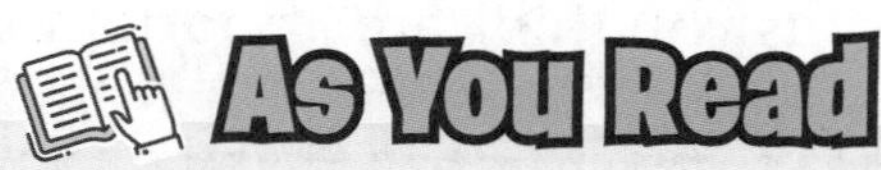

Put parentheses around words you think are important vocabulary in the text.

A Popular Sport

Soccer is one of the most popular sports in the world. In many other countries, including Brazil, soccer is not called *soccer*. It's called *football*. But whatever you call it, soccer is a thrilling game.

Soccer has several rules. First, soccer teams have 11 players. Players use their feet and sometimes their heads to move the ball toward the goal. To score a goal, a soccer team has to kick the ball into the other team's goal. The goalie's job is to stop the ball from getting in the goal, and they can touch the ball with their hands or arms. If players do not follow the rules, they can get penalties. This includes yellow and red cards. To win the game, one team has to score more goals than the other team.

1. Which is a synonym for *thrilling*?
   - (A) new
   - (B) boring
   - (C) difficult
   - (D) exciting

2. Which word uses a suffix that means "someone who"?
   - (A) soccer
   - (B) popular
   - (C) player
   - (D) whatever

3. How is a goal scored in soccer?

____

____

4. How might soccer be different if all players could touch the ball with their hands?

____

____

Name: ______________________ Date: ______________

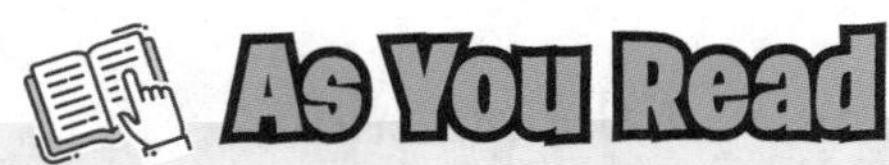

Put parentheses around words you think are important vocabulary in the text.

Welcome to Brazil!

Welcome to Brazil! Big, exciting cities can be found across the country. There are also beautiful beaches. The largest river in the world is there. The largest rain forest in the world is also there. And the sport of soccer is very popular. There are many things to see and do in this country.

Brazil's geography and weather is unique. Brazil is a large country. In fact, it is the largest country in South America. It is south of the equator, so the seasons are different from countries that are north of the equator. For example, July is a winter month in Brazil. In the United States, July is a summer month. The northern part of Brazil has a tropical climate. The southern part of Brazil has a cooler climate.

The Amazon River and the Amazon Rain Forest can be found in the northern part of Brazil. The Amazon River is one of the world's largest rivers. It flows into the Atlantic Ocean. It adds a lot of fresh water to the ocean. The Amazon River goes through the Amazon Rain Forest. This forest has many plants and animals. It is home to more than one-half of the world's species of plants and animals. Many important resources, such as trees and water, are found in the Amazon.

Brazil has a lot of big cities. The capital is near the center of the country. It is called *Brasilia*. Many other big cities are along the coast. They have beautiful beaches. There are fun things for people to do. Rio de Janeiro is one of those big cities. Carnival is very popular time of year in Rio. During this holiday, there are big parades. There are big parties. The people dress in fancy costumes. They listen to music and dance.

Soccer is a very popular sport in Brazil. It is called *football* there. Many people in Brazil are good at this game. Some of them become very famous. They go on to play for professional football teams. For fun, many people in Brazil like to watch football matches. They like to watch their favorite teams on TV.

Brazil has a lot to offer. If you visit the country, maybe you will see some of these things, too!

Name: ______________________________ Date: ______________

Directions: Read "Welcome to Brazil!" Then, answer the questions.

1. Which sentence best describes the text's purpose?
   - (A) The text was written to instruct.
   - (B) The text was written to persuade.
   - (C) The text was written to inform.
   - (D) The text was written to entertain.

2. Which title does **not** provide enough information to make a prediction about the text?
   - (A) The Amazon River
   - (B) The Amazon Rain Forest
   - (C) Soccer—A Sport of the World
   - (D) all of the above

3. People who like _____ would most likely read the text.
   - (A) cooking
   - (B) mathematics
   - (C) history
   - (D) travel

4. Which is **not** true about Carnival?
   - (A) Many plays are performed.
   - (B) There are parades.
   - (C) People wear costumes.
   - (D) There are big parties.

5. Write one fact from the text about each topic.

Amazon River	
Amazon Rain Forest	
seasons	
cities	
football	

Name: ______________________________ Date: ________________

Directions: Reread "Welcome to Brazil!" Then, respond to the prompt.

Imagine you work for the tourism department in Brazil. Write a paragraph to convince readers to visit Brazil. Include at least three reasons they should visit. Use details from the text to support your reasons. Include an introduction and a conclusion sentence.

Name: ______________________________ Date: ______________

Directions: Read the text, and answer the questions.

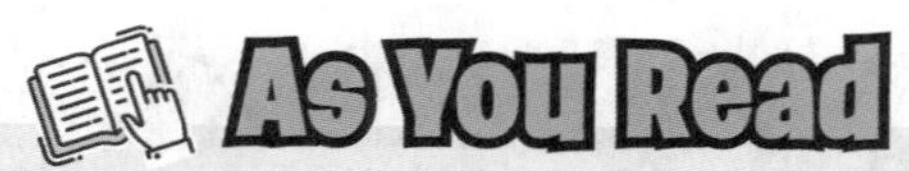

Circle words and phrases that tell you about the main character.

Pal from Brazil

Alex had lots of friends, and they were all pretty predictable. They liked the same movies, video games, and food. They talked about the same stuff all the time. That was both good and bad. He liked the familiarity, but sometimes, he got bored.

One day at school, Alex saw a notice on the bulletin board that said, "Join our new pen pal program. Meet someone from another country!"

A new friend could be interesting, he thought to himself. Alex asked his teacher about it, and he found out that the program would connect him with someone his own age who spoke English.

"That sounds great," Alex said. "When can I start writing letters?"

"You'll have to pick a country first," his teacher told him. "And you won't be writing letters like back in my day—you'll be writing emails!"

What country should I pick? Alex thought to himself. He remembered that his mother sometimes went to Brazil for business trips, so he picked that country. *Brazil is probably cool*, he thought.

1. How will Alex communicate with his pen pal?
   - (A) letters
   - (B) texting
   - (C) emails
   - (D) phone calls

2. How should the word *different* be broken into syllables?
   - (A) dif·fer·ent
   - (B) di·ffer·ent
   - (C) diff·er·ent
   - (D) differ·ent

3. Why does Alex choose a pen pal from Brazil?
   - (A) Students speak English.
   - (B) It is his only choice.
   - (C) His friends chose Brazil.
   - (D) His mom travels there for work.

4. What is the root word in *predictable*?
   - (A) *–able*
   - (B) *predict*
   - (C) *pre–*
   - (D) *–ict*

Name: ______________________________ Date: ________________

Directions: Read the text, and answer the questions.

Circle at least five words with a prefix or suffix.

His Pal Paulo

Paulo was the name of Alex's pen pal. Alex was so excited to write to him. But he wasn't sure how to begin his email. Alex thought to himself. *Maybe I should tell him about myself first.*

Alex first wrote, *Hi, Paulo*, and he paused. Then he wrote his name and his age, what grade he was in, and what he liked about his favorite sports teams. After that, he ran out of things to say, so he sent the email.

A couple of days later, Paulo emailed him back! His email began:

Hi Alex,

I live in Rio de Janeiro, the second-biggest city in Brazil. It's nice to meet you, my new friend.

Alex couldn't contain his excitement. He read the rest of Paulo's email eagerly, learning about Paulo's favorite soccer team and what his family was like. Paulo also wanted to know more about Alex and his family. Paulo ended by asking what life was like in the United States.

Alex thought, *Wow! My buddies and I never talk about this stuff.*

1. Which word has a suffix?

Ⓐ begin
Ⓑ life
Ⓒ soccer
Ⓓ biggest

2. What does Paulo want to learn about?

Ⓐ Alex's life
Ⓑ cities in the United States
Ⓒ Rio de Janeiro
Ⓓ soccer

3. How many syllables are in the word *favorite*?

Ⓐ one
Ⓑ two
Ⓒ three
Ⓓ four

4. Which word best describes Paulo?

Ⓐ silly
Ⓑ curious
Ⓒ brave
Ⓓ adventurous

Name: ______________________________ Date: ______________

Directions: Read the text, and answer the questions.

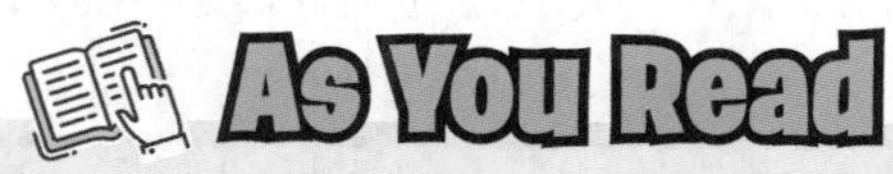

Circle words and phrases that tell you about the characters' relationship.

Alex Learns a Lot

Soon, Alex and Paulo were writing emails to each other every few days. They were learning more and more about each other. There were so many questions to ask: What kind of music do you like? What are your favorite movies and video games? What foods do you hate and love? Do you have pets? What do kids in your country do after school? What is your neighborhood like?

They talked about stories that were in the news in both of their countries. Alex was learning a lot about Paulo and his home, and it seemed like Paulo was learning a lot about the United States.

Paulo made his home city of Rio sound like an amazing place. Paulo lived near a beach and went swimming year-round. His wardrobe consisted of shorts, T-shirts, and flip-flops.

I'd love to visit Rio one day, wrote Alex.

Little did he know, his wish was about to come true!

1. Based on the last sentence, what will most likely happen next?
   - (A) Paulo will come to Alex's city.
   - (B) Alex will go to Rio.
   - (C) Paulo will stop writing letters.
   - (D) Alex will send Paul a picture.

2. How should the word *awesome* be broken into syllables?
   - (A) awe·some
   - (B) a·we·some
   - (C) aw·e·some
   - (D) awes·ome

3. What is the climate like in Rio? What clues in the text let you know?

____

____

4. What are some questions you would ask Paulo if you could?

____

____

Name: ______________________________ Date: ______________

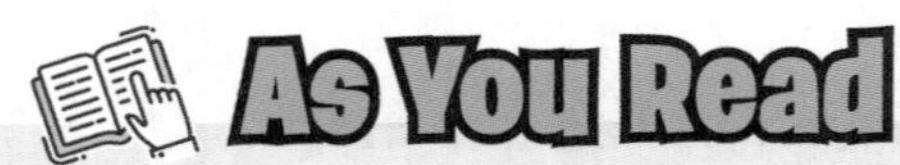

Circle at least eight words with a prefix or suffix.

Rio Rocks!

"Get packed, Alex. We're going to Rio!" said Alex's mother. She was going there for work and taking Alex with her. Alex was pumped. Right away, he emailed Paulo with the news.

Two days later, Alex and his mom landed in Rio. At the hotel, Alex got in touch with Paulo. Paulo, Alex, and their moms met in the hotel lobby. They got along immediately. Paulo and Alex hugged.

Alex and his mom went with Paulo and Marta, Paulo's mom, on a quick bus ride to one of the world's most famous beaches, Copacabana. It was a long stretch of white sand packed with people.

"This is the place to see Cariocas," said Paulo.

"Is that some kind of fish?" asked Alex.

"Cariocas are people from Rio," said Paulo, chuckling.

Some men and women were playing volleyball on a section of the beach.

"Let's play!" said Paulo. But the game didn't last long. The Brazilians were great players. Paulo and Alex lost two straight games without winning a point!

After lunch, they headed for Ipanema, another famous beach. There, Alex took his first swim in the waters off South America.

Paulo liked showing off his city. After the beach, they took a bus back to the city and walked through Tijuca National Park.

"No other city has a forest this big in it," said Paulo. Alex was amazed to see monkeys, sloths, and all kinds of exotic birds in the park.

Over the next week, they checked out other sights: Sugar Loaf Mountain, a giant statue of Christ, big buildings, and great museums. But Alex was happiest hitting the beaches. There were lots of them! Alex also enjoyed the Brazilian food he ate. He loved feijoada. This was a stew that had black beans, meat, and vegetables. Alex drank juice from fruits he had never heard of. He ate fried cod balls and other tasty dishes. Everything was delicious!

Too soon, the trip was ending. Alex didn't want to leave. But as it turned out, Paulo's family was going to come visit the United States next year.

Alex said to Paulo, "I can't wait to show you the sights, pal!"

Name: ______________________________ Date: ________________

Directions: Read "Rio Rocks!" Then, answer the questions.

1. What is the suffix in *ending*?

(A) *–ding*
(B) *–end*
(C) *–ng*
(D) *–ing*

2. What are Cariocas?

(A) people from Rio
(B) Brazilian fish
(C) famous beaches
(D) stew with black beans

3. Which is an example of a compound word?

(A) volleyball
(B) favorite
(C) national
(D) vegetables

4. Why does Alex visit Brazil?

(A) His soccer team was traveling there for a tournament.
(B) His mom was traveling there for work.
(C) His family went there on vacation.
(D) His dad got a new job there.

5. Use the text to complete the chart and describe Alex's activities in Brazil.

Beaches	City Sights	Food

Name: ______________________ Date: ______________

Directions: Reread "Rio Rocks!" Then, respond to the prompt.

Imagine you are matched with a pen pal. Write an introductory letter to them. Be sure to write information about yourself and where you live. Ask your pen pal a few questions about themselves.

Name: ______________________________ Date: ________________

World Almanac

BRAZIL

Brazil is the largest country in South America. Only four countries in the world are larger than Brazil. The borders of all but two countries in South America touch Brazil. A country this size has lots of attractions. Brazil has the biggest city in South America. It has the world's largest rain forest. The land and its people are diverse. Most of its people live in large cities. The climate is warm. And the beaches are beautiful. No wonder so many people love to visit Brazil!

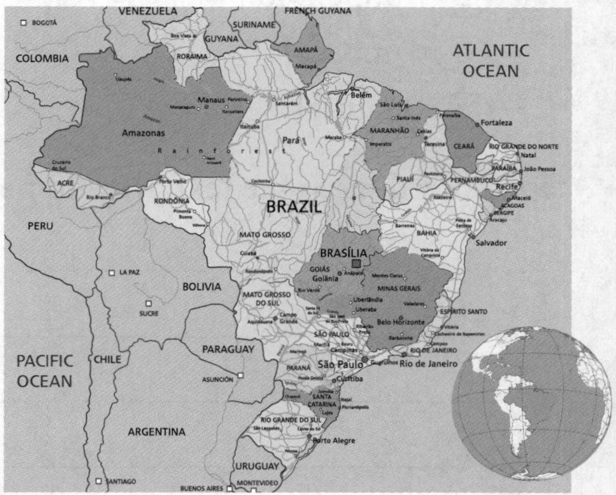

Location: South America

Area: 3,286,470 square miles (8,515,770 square kilometers)

Population: 217,240,060 (estimate as of 2022)

Government: federal presidential republic

Capital: Brasilia

Other major cities: São Paulo, Rio de Janeiro, Salvador

Languages: Portuguese (official), Spanish, English, French

Currency: real

Longest river: Amazon River, 3,976 miles (6,400 kilometers)

Highest point: Pico da Neblina, 9,888 feet (3,014 meters)

Climate: mostly tropical

Major industries: textiles, shoes, chemicals, cement, lumber, iron ore, tin, steel, aircraft

Natural resources: gold, platinum, tin, rare earth elements, uranium, petroleum

Name: ______________________________ Date: ______________

Directions: Read "Brazil." Then, answer the questions.

1. Where do most people live in Brazil?
   - (A) Amazon Rain Forest
   - (B) beaches
   - (C) rural farmland
   - (D) large cities

2. Which word has a prefix?
   - (A) largest
   - (B) population
   - (C) unusual
   - (D) natural

3. Which is **not** a language of Brazil?
   - (A) French
   - (B) Italian
   - (C) Portuguese
   - (D) Spanish

4. How many syllables are in *variety*?
   - (A) three
   - (B) one
   - (C) four
   - (D) two

5. According to the text, why do people visit Brazil?

____

____

____

____

Name: ______________________________ Date: ______________

Directions: Read these texts. Then, reread the almanac page about Brazil on page 77. Use the table to take notes about what each text shows about Brazil

Close-Reading Texts

An Important Rain Forest	Rio Rocks!
The Amazon Rain Forest is a special place. It is a tropical rain forest. That means it gets very warm. It also gets a lot of rain. It gets over 59 inches (150 centimeters) of rain per year! This is a lot more than most places on Earth. Also, the Amazon is home to one-half of the world's species. Many unique plants and animals live there.	Alex and his mom went with Paulo and Marta, Paulo's mom, on a quick bus ride to one of the world's most famous beaches, Copacabana. It was a long stretch of white sand packed with people. "This is the place to see Cariocas," said Paulo. "Is that some kind of fish?" asked Alex. "Cariocas are people from Rio," said Paulo, chuckling.

An Important Rain Forest	Rio Rocks!	Brazil

Name: ______________________ Date: ______________

Directions: Read these texts. Then, use the Venn diagram to compare and contrast how Rio de Janeiro is described in each.

Close-Reading Texts

Welcome to Brazil	Rio Rocks!
Brazil has a lot of big cities. Many of those cities are on the coast. They have beautiful beaches. There are fun things to do. Rio de Janeiro is one of those big cities. Carnival is very popular in Rio. There are big parades. There are big parties. The people dress in fancy costumes. They listen to music and dance.	Paulo liked showing off his city. After the beach, they took a bus back to the city and walked through Tijuca National Park. "No other city has a forest this big in it," said Paulo. Alex was amazed to see monkeys, sloths, and all kinds of exotic birds in the park. Over the next week, they checked out other sights: Sugar Loaf Mountain, a giant statue of Christ, big buildings, and great museums. But Alex was happiest hitting the beaches.

Welcome to Brazil **Rio Rocks!**

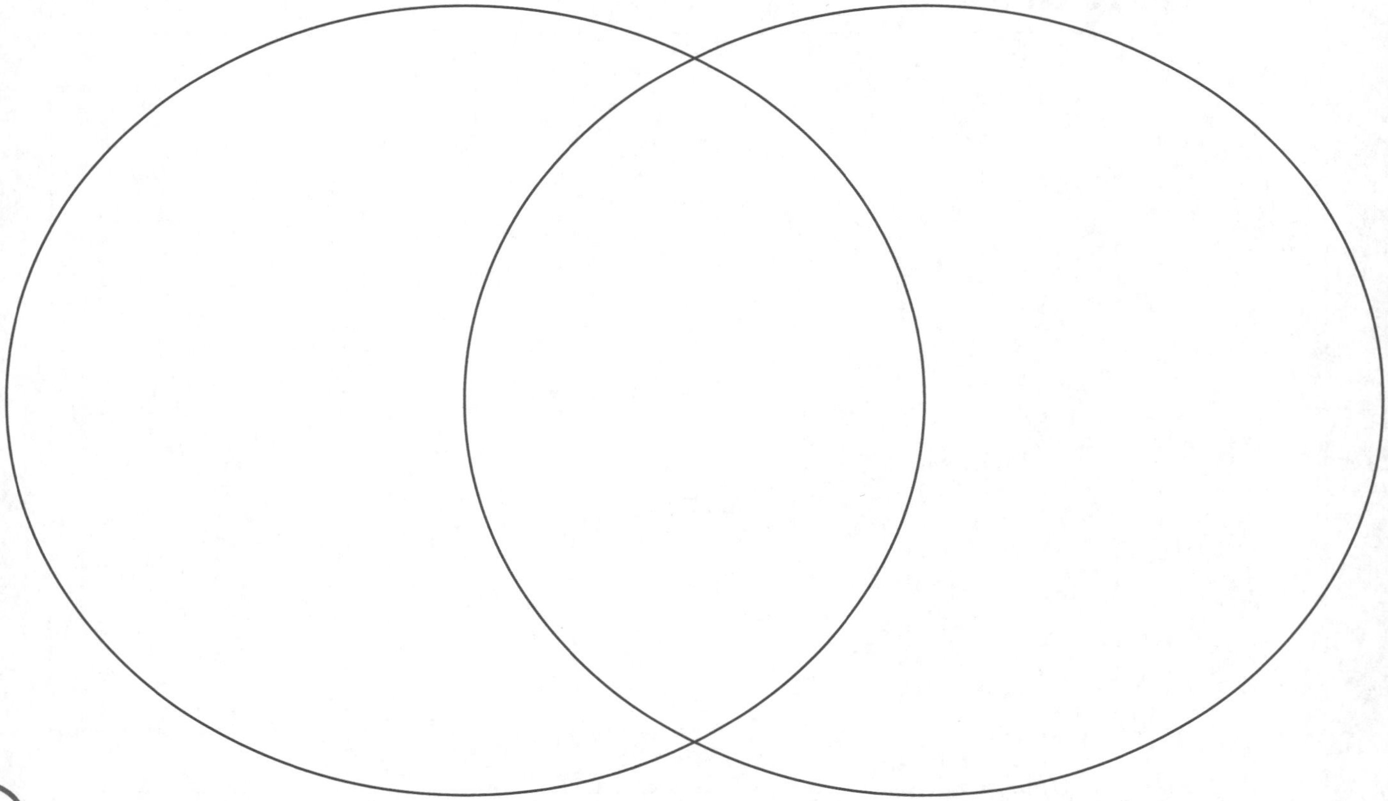

Name: ______________________ Date: ______________

Directions: Think about the text from this unit. Then, respond to the prompt.

Write a paragraph about Brazil. Use information from the texts and fact list. Remember to include introduction and conclusion sentences.

Name: ______________________________ Date: ______________

Directions: Choose a country you would like to learn more about. Use a book or an online resource to research the country. Write a paragraph about the country and complete the fact list. Draw a picture.

Country: ______________________________

Location ______________________________

Population: ______________________________

Capital: ______________________________

Languages: ______________________________

Money: ______________________________

Longest river: ______________________________

Highest point: ______________________________

Climate: ______________________________

Natural resources: ______________________________

Name: ______________________________ Date: ______________

Directions: Read the text, and answer the questions.

Underline the main idea of the paragraph.

The Mystery of the Red Planet

Look up in the sky right after the sun sets. You can see a bright object close to the horizon. This is the planet Mars. Mars is one of five planets you don't need a telescope to see. What makes Mars really stand out is its red color. The ancient Romans named Mars after their god of war. That's because red is the color of blood. Of course, Mars does not have blood on it. The planet's red color comes from the reddish dust that covers the ground. Because of this dust, Mars has been nicknamed the Red Planet. Mars is pretty close to Earth, so it has fascinated humans throughout history. Of all the mysteries about Mars, the biggest one is this: Is there life on this planet?

1. Mars is the only planet that ______.

- (A) is named by Romans
- (B) is red
- (C) can be seen without a telescope
- (D) is near Earth

2. What makes Mars look red?

- (A) rock
- (B) blood
- (C) dust
- (D) sunlight

3. How should *ancient* be broken into syllables?

- (A) anc·ient
- (B) an·cient
- (C) a·ncient
- (D) anci·ent

4. What is the purpose of this text?

- (A) to entertain
- (B) to persuade
- (C) to scare
- (D) to inform

Name: ______________________________ Date: ______________

Directions: Read the text, and answer the questions.

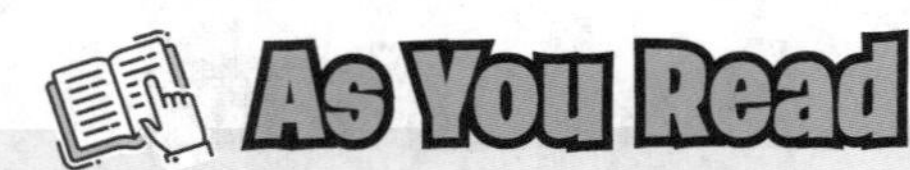

Underline the main idea of the text.

Intelligent Life

Since the telescope was invented, people have aimed it at Mars. Early observers made maps of the planet. They drew the different features they saw. In the late 1800s, one observer said he saw canals on the planet. He thought they were rivers of water. One scientist said that intelligent beings built the canals. This idea inspired many authors. They wrote stories about beings that lived on Mars. The most famous was called *The War of the Worlds*. It was written by H. G. Wells. His book was made into a movie. Since then, there have been plenty of other books and movies about Martians. These Martians were often shown as monsters attacking Earth.

Today, no life on Mars has been found. But still, people are interested in the planet. They hope to find that life may have existed there in the past.

1. What does *observer* mean?
   - (A) a person who watches something
   - (B) a person who follows important events
   - (C) a person who creates drawings
   - (D) a person who studies space

2. Why did people believe there was life on Mars?
   - (A) They saw Martians.
   - (B) They wrote stories about Martians.
   - (C) They thought Martians built canals.
   - (D) They got letters from Martians.

3. What is the main idea of the text?
   - (A) Scientists believed there was life on Mars.
   - (B) Books written about Mars are interesting.
   - (C) People have been interested in Mars for a long time.
   - (D) Telescopes taught people about Mars.

4. Which word has a suffix?
   - (A) early
   - (B) telescope
   - (C) plenty
   - (D) attacking

Name: ______________________________ Date: ________________

Directions: Read the text, and answer the questions.

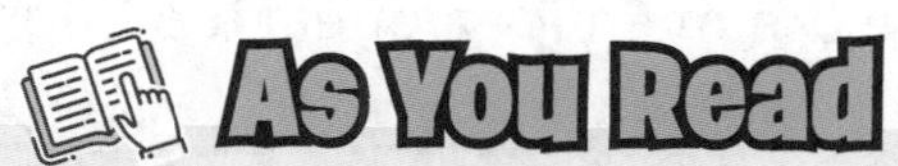

Underline the main idea of each paragraph.

Robots on Mars

Martian surface

Several spacecrafts have been sent to explore Mars. NASA is the group in charge of them. NASA is a U.S. government organization. Some of NASA's spacecrafts flew past Mars. Other spacecrafts flew around Mars. And some spacecrafts even landed on Mars!

These spacecrafts have made amazing discoveries. They photographed incredible sights. One is a volcano larger than any on Earth. Another is a giant canyon ten times longer than the Grand Canyon.

NASA also landed machines on the surface of the planet. These machines are called rovers. They are laboratories on wheels. Rovers have explored parts of Mars. They have drilled into rocks to see what they are made of. When dust storms happened, they recorded them. Rovers also measured the air quality. Finally, rovers have searched for signs of water. Rovers have taken pictures of dry riverbeds and rounded pebbles. These were made by flowing water long ago. Scientists believe liquid water is needed for life to exist. Was there once life on Mars? Rovers are still working to find out.

1. Which is a compound word?
   - (A) recorded
   - (B) spacecraft
   - (C) photographed
   - (D) volcano

2. Which object is considered a laboratory on wheels?
   - (A) spacecraft
   - (B) rover
   - (C) probe
   - (D) camera

3. Why are rounded pebbles a clue that there was once flowing water?

   ____

4. Which rover job do you think is most important? Why?

   ____

   ____

Name: ______________________________ Date: ____________________

Underline the main idea of each paragraph.

Expedition to Mars

So far, only machines have landed on Mars. But NASA hopes to change that. They want to send a piloted expedition to Mars in about 20 years. This might seem like a dangerous trip, but it is an important one. One of NASA's goals is to learn whether Mars once held life. Experts think only human explorers can answer that question.

NASA has other goals as well. The trip will increase scientific knowledge. Setting foot on Mars will inspire the nation and the world. Young people will want to study more science and math. New technology created for the expedition will benefit everyone. And learning more about Mars could mean that people could live there someday. Out of all the planets in the solar system, only Mars could be another home for humans. Scientists want to learn if living sustainably on Mars is possible.

NASA hopes to first build a base on the moon. They'll use that knowledge to build a base on Mars. The ship taking humans to Mars will hold four astronauts. The spacecraft will orbit Mars, and two astronauts will rocket down to the surface. They will work for 30 days. Tons of food and equipment will be sent ahead by robots. A fueled rocket will also be waiting on Mars. When the 30 days are up, the astronauts will use it to reunite with the orbiting ship.

This mission has some challenges. The round trip will take about 500 days. There will be little gravity on the ship. So, the astronauts' muscles and bones will become weak. Also, it is difficult to live in a small space for a long time. This might affect the emotions of the astronauts. But NASA is trying to understand the effects of this type of isolation. They are placing astronauts in a sealed habitat for a year to see how they react.

NASA isn't the only group hoping to reach Mars. China has landed a rover on Mars. It says it will send humans to Mars in the 2030s. And some private spaceflight companies that are not funded by the government have also set their sights on Mars. One company promises to send a million people to Mars by the end of the twenty-first century. People hope to find out if Mars once held life. They also want to find out if it can be our second home!

Name: ______________________________ Date: ______________

Directions: Read “Expedition to Mars.” Then, answer the questions.

1. What is the first step in sending people to Mars?
   - (A) sending food and supplies
   - (B) building a base on the moon
   - (C) fueling a rocket for reuniting
   - (D) building a base on Mars

2. Which word is a person who will explore?
   - (A) explorer
   - (B) exploring
   - (C) explored
   - (D) explores

3. Which country is **not** trying to send humans to Mars?
   - (A) China
   - (B) France
   - (C) United States
   - (D) private spaceflight companies

4. What does private mean in the phrase private spaceflight companies?
   - (A) They are very expensive.
   - (B) They are a low military rank.
   - (C) No one knows about them.
   - (D) They are not funded by the government.

5. Complete the web using information from the text.

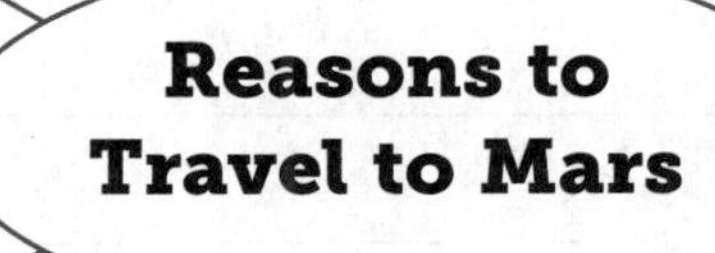

Name: ______________________ **Date:** ______________

Directions: Reread "Expedition to Mars." Then, respond to the prompt.

Write a summary of the text. Remember, a summary should include only the most important details from a piece of writing. The ideas should be written in your own words. Your summary should be at least four sentences.

Name: ______________________________ Date: ________________

Directions: Read the text, and answer the questions.

Underline words or phrases that show emotion.

Leaving Earth

Josh felt anxious. He had never left Earth before. And he had never been to the moon or to Mars. Seated in a spacecraft, Josh was about to do all three things.

A screen in the cabin counted down from ten.

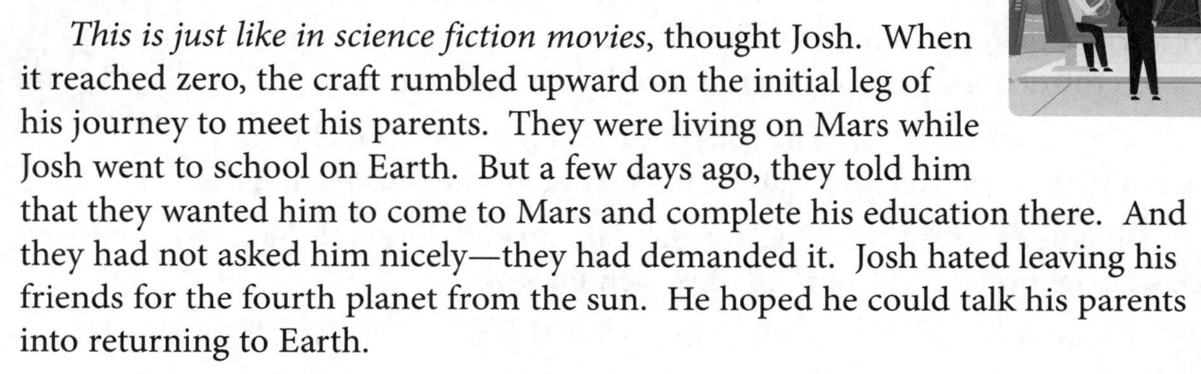

This is just like in science fiction movies, thought Josh. When it reached zero, the craft rumbled upward on the initial leg of his journey to meet his parents. They were living on Mars while Josh went to school on Earth. But a few days ago, they told him that they wanted him to come to Mars and complete his education there. And they had not asked him nicely—they had demanded it. Josh hated leaving his friends for the fourth planet from the sun. He hoped he could talk his parents into returning to Earth.

Josh got off at the U.S. Lunar Base to switch spacecrafts. There was no time for sightseeing on the moon, so he quickly boarded the Mars Express. Soon enough, he was blasting off to Mars.

1. Which word best describes how Josh feels about going to Mars?

- (A) confident
- (B) unhappy
- (C) bored
- (D) excited

2. Why is Josh going to Mars?

- (A) to complete his education
- (B) to be in a movie
- (C) to build a lunar base
- (D) to vacation and sightsee

3. Which word is a synonym of *demanded*?

- (A) asked
- (B) replied
- (C) encouraged
- (D) required

4. What genre would this story fit?

- (A) historical fiction
- (B) fantasy
- (C) science fiction
- (D) realistic fiction

Name: ______________________________ Date: ______________

Directions: Read the text, and answer the questions.

Underline words or phrases that show emotion.

Landing on Mars

The trip to Mars took six months. The food was dull, and the quarters were cramped. Still, Josh felt relieved that the trip was uneventful.

But one day, as he was working on his math homework, a computer voice blared, "Solar flare alert! Proceed to station nine!"

Josh jumped up from his table. At station nine, everyone on board crowded into a room surrounded by water-filled tanks.

A crew member said, "The solar flare will pass us in one hour. The radiation could fry us, but the tanks should shield us from harm."

Josh gulped nervously. Luckily, the flare missed the ship! But it was eerie to see its bright red glow from the ship's windows.

With no other incidents, the ship reached Mars. Josh's parents greeted him.

"We'll take you home to Beta Colony," said his father. "You'll love it there."

But Josh missed fresh air, and he felt miserable. Outside the walls, he would die instantly in Mars' deadly atmosphere. He missed Earth already.

1. Which word best describes the spacecraft?
   - (A) boring
   - (B) luxurious
   - (C) dangerous
   - (D) entertaining

2. Which is true about the word *uneventful*?
   - (A) It has a prefix and a suffix.
   - (B) It doesn't have a prefix or suffix.
   - (C) It only has a suffix.
   - (D) It only has a prefix.

3. What does the word *cramped* mean?
   - (A) a type of tool
   - (B) solar flares
   - (C) restrictive and small
   - (D) not allowing freedom

4. What danger does Josh face on Mars?
   - (A) cramped quarters
   - (B) Martians
   - (C) lack of water and food
   - (D) deadly atmosphere

Name: ______________________________ Date: ________________

Directions: Read the text, and answer the questions.

Underline words or phrases that show emotion.

A New Home

At his new home, Josh learned that people born on Mars were called Martians, while people who were born on Earth were called *Outerlings*.

On his first day in school, Josh looked at the schedule on the board and asked, "Why isn't Earth history being taught?"

"Because we don't live on Earth, Outerling," sneered a student. Everyone snickered, and Josh blushed as red as the dirt outside the class window.

By the end of the school day, Josh really hated Mars! He was standing in line for the bus when a Martian student approached him.

"Hey, I'm Cody," he said. "Not everyone here gives Outerlings a hard time."

He offered Josh a tour of the colony. The highlight was a large domed building.

"They grow fruit and vegetables here," Cody said.

"Animals use up too many resources, but we get protein from insects we raise. You could try a grasshopper burger," Cody said. "It tastes kind of nutty."

"I'm good, thanks," laughed Josh.

1. What is an Outerling?

- (A) a person born on Mars
- (B) a person who lives outside the colony
- (C) a person born on Earth
- (D) a new person at school

2. Which word best describes Cody?

- (A) funny
- (B) curious
- (C) friendly
- (D) intelligent

3. How is school different on Mars than on Earth?

____

4. Based on this text, what difficulties could Josh have on Mars?

____

Name: ____________________ Date: ______________

Underline words or phrases that show emotion.

A New Discovery

"I'm going on an expedition tomorrow with one of my friends," said Cody. "Want to join us?"

"Absolutely," replied Josh.

The next day, Josh put on a light space suit. A large rover pulled up with Cody's friends. Josh asked if they ever wanted to visit Earth. A girl named Demos said, "No way. Our families are pioneers, and they're building a better world than Earth."

Josh asked, "But can you survive without water?"

Cody replied, "Nope. All our water comes from Earth in cargo rockets. It's expensive, and I don't know how long they can keep bringing it to us."

Suddenly, the rover slowed to a stop. Cody went outside to wipe dust off the solar panels. A moment later he returned and excitedly said, "Looks like a recent Marsquake left an opening in the canyon wall!"

"It looks like a lava tube," Cody said.

"It must have been made millions of years ago," Demos said.

The group entered the tube and walked down a tunnel, lit by their suit lights. The walls began to glisten in the light. Looking at them closely, Josh realized they were made of ice! Cody and Demos could hardly believe it.

A trickle of water dripped from the walls, flowing along the ground and down the tunnel. They followed the little river. Minutes later, they saw something shimmering up ahead. It was a large lake of water. At the far end of the lake, water gushed down through an opening in the rocky wall.

"There's water on Mars after all!" Cody yelled.

Name: ______________________________ Date: ________________

Directions: Read "A New Discovery." Then, answer the questions.

1. Which word is a synonym of *pioneer*?
   - (A) leader
   - (B) student
   - (C) traveler
   - (D) explorer

2. Which suffix makes sense with the word *deep*?
   - (A) *–en*
   - (B) *–s*
   - (C) *–ing*
   - (D) *–ed*

3. How does Demos feel about living on Mars?
   - (A) jealous
   - (B) adventurous
   - (C) proud
   - (D) ashamed

4. What is a *Marsquake*?
   - (A) flooding on Mars
   - (B) a big wind storm on Mars
   - (C) an eruption of a volcano on Mars
   - (D) the shaking of Mars' surface

5. Write information to describe elements of the story.

Characters	Setting	Plot

Unit 5
WEEK 2
DAY
5

Name: ______________________________ Date: ______________

Directions: Reread "A New Discovery." Then, respond to the prompt.

Demos told Josh he might end up in a history book because he discovered water on Mars. Write a paragraph that could be found in a history book for future Martian students to read. Be sure to explain who Josh is and what he did to help life on Mars. Draw a picture to support your writing.

MARS PATROL

A MARS BETA COLONY SECURITY FORCE IS ON ITS DAILY PATROL.

"Unit 5, head for Kasei. A climber is stuck."

"Not another! They never learn."

"I hope our rope ladder is long enough."

THE PATROL REACHES THE DEEP CHANNEL CALLED KASEI VALLIS.

NEAR THE PATROL, A DUST STORM LOOMS.

Name: ______________________________ Date: ________________

Directions: Read "Mars Patrol." Then, answer the questions.

1. Why do the police go on patrol?

Ⓐ to rescue a climber
Ⓑ to locate a dust storm
Ⓒ to repair solar panels
Ⓓ to practice missions

2. What is the prefix in the word *recharge*?

Ⓐ *rec–*
Ⓑ *–arge*
Ⓒ *–ge*
Ⓓ *re–*

3. Which word is a synonym for *predicament*?

Ⓐ rover
Ⓑ dust storm
Ⓒ solution
Ⓓ problem

4. Which inference makes the most sense?

Ⓐ The police are good at their jobs.
Ⓑ The police are frustrated at the climber.
Ⓒ The climber is brave.
Ⓓ The climber will save the cops.

5. What is the problem in the story?

____

____

____

____

Name: ______________________ Date: ______________

Directions: Closely read these texts. Then reread "Mars Patrol" on page 95. Take notes in the table of descriptions about Mars.

Close-Reading Texts

Robots on Mars	Landing on Mars
Rovers have explored parts of Mars. They have drilled into rocks to see what they are made of. When dust storms happened, they recorded them. Rovers also measured the air quality. Finally, rovers have searched for signs of water. Rovers have taken pictures of dry riverbeds and rounded pebbles. These were made by flowing water long ago.	"We'll take you home to Beta Colony," said his father. "You'll love it there." But Josh missed fresh air, and he felt miserable. Outside the walls, he would die instantly in Mars' deadly atmosphere. He missed Earth already.

Robots on Mars	
Landing on Mars	
Mars Patrol	

Name: ______________________________ Date: ________________

Directions: Closely read these texts. Use the table to compare and contrast the trips to Mars described in each.

Close-Reading Texts

Expedition to Mars	Landing on Mars
This mission has some challenges. The round trip will take about 500 days. There will be little gravity on the ship. So, the astronauts' muscles and bones will become weak. Also, it is difficult to live in a small space for a long time. This might affect the emotions of the astronauts. But NASA is trying to understand the effects of this type of isolation. They are placing astronauts in a sealed habitat for a year to see how they react.	The trip to Mars took six months, but it seemed longer. The food was dull, and the quarters were cramped. Still, Josh felt relieved that the trip was uneventful. But one day, as he was working on his math homework, a computer voice blared, "Solar flare alert! Proceed to station nine!" Josh jumped up from his table.

	Expedition to Mars	Landing on Mars
Length of Trip		
Possible Dangers		

Both

Name: ______________________ **Date:** ______________

Directions: Reread "Mars Patrol." Then, respond to the prompt.

The climber needed to be rescued. Use your imagination to write a short story about the climber before the patrol officers came to help him. Before you write, think about these questions: Why was he out there? How did he get stuck? What was his goal? Your story should have a beginning and middle. It should end with the climber stuck on the side of the trench.

Name: ______________________________ Date: ______________

Directions: Create the next four frames for the graphic novel, "Mars Patrol." Write the text and draw the pictures for your new part of the story.

Name: ______________________ Date: ______________

Directions: Read the text, and answer the questions.

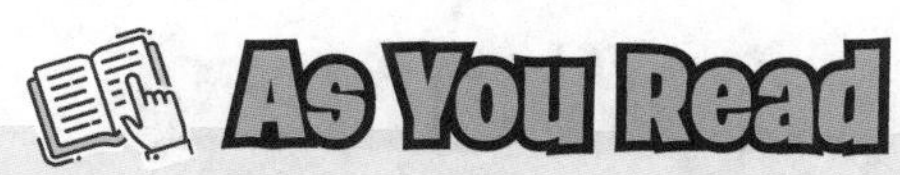

Look for and underline examples of compare and contrast in the text.

The Importance of Vacations

Do you like to go on vacations? Vacations can be relaxing and a lot of fun. You can travel to new places, try new things, and meet new people. But did you know that vacations are good for you? It's true! Vacations allow you to rest, and rest is very important because it keeps you healthy. Rest supports your body and your mind by helping you think better and improving your mood. Vacations provide much more than just rest, though. They also allow you to jump, run, swim, and play. Being active is very good for you. When you move your body, you help your body stay healthy. Vacations also let you do things you enjoy. When you do things you enjoy doing, you feel happy, and feeling happy is good for you. So, the next time you're feeling run-down and overwhelmed, think about whether you need a vacation!

1. What is the main idea?
   - (A) Being active is healthy.
   - (B) Vacations are good for you.
   - (C) Rest helps you think better.
   - (D) Vacations are a lot of fun.

2. Which is the suffix in vacation?
   - (A) *-on*
   - (B) *vacate-*
   - (C) *-tion*
   - (D) *vaca-*

3. Which words are synonyms?
   - (A) rest and active
   - (B) mood and move
   - (C) also and allow
   - (D) rest and relax

4. Which reason for taking a vacation is **not** given in the text?
   - (A) You can miss school or work.
   - (B) Your body can rest.
   - (C) You can do meet new people.
   - (D) You can be active.

Name: ______________________________ **Date:** ________________

Directions: Read the text, and answer the questions.

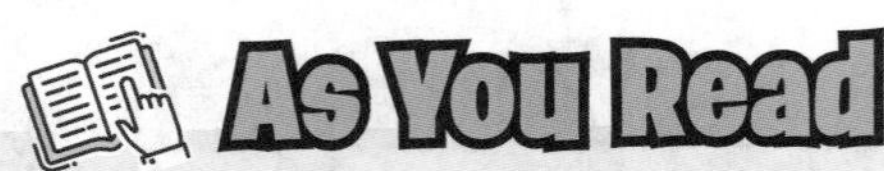

Look for and underline examples of compare and contrast in the text.

Vacation Variety

There are many different kinds of vacations and even more things to do on vacation. Some people like to be outdoors. Hiking and camping are good vacations for these people. Other people like to go swimming. They like warm weather and sandy beaches. People who like sun, sand, and the perfect place to swim often go to the ocean. Some people prefer big cities. They like to visit museums and go to restaurants. They like to shop and go to plays and movies. Finally, some people have big families that they like to visit. When they go on vacation, they spend time with their families. What about you? What kind of vacation would you like to have?

1. Which definition of *plays* is used in the text?

- (A) dramatic performances
- (B) exercise activities
- (C) works
- (D) amusements

2. Swimming, hiking, and camping share the same _____.

- (A) root word
- (B) prefix
- (C) meaning
- (D) suffix

3. *Sun, sand, and swimming* is an example of _____.

- (A) alliteration
- (B) a simile
- (C) a rhyme
- (D) a metaphor

4. In which chapter would you most likely find the text above?

- (A) Chapter 5: Vacations in the Big City
- (B) Chapter 7: Outdoor Fun
- (C) Chapter 3: Choosing the Vacation Destination for You
- (D) Chapter 12: Hawai'i's Vacation Hot Spots

Name: ______________________________ Date: ________________

Directions: Read the text, and answer the questions.

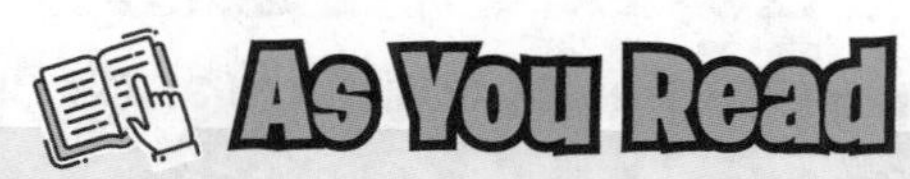

Look for and underline examples of compare and contrast in the text.

Packing for Vacation

What should you take with you on vacation? That depends on where you are going. One key tip is to research what the weather will be like at the place you are visiting. That way, you can bring the right kind of clothes.

Here are a few guidelines you can follow for what to pack. Suppose you are going to the beach. Swimsuits, shorts, and beach towels will be important, and you'll need sunscreen, too. If you are going hiking or camping, you will need different supplies, such as sturdy shoes, long pants, and a jacket. Plus, don't forget the bug spray since you will be outdoors often! If you are going to a big city, make sure you bring comfortable shoes. You will probably be walking a lot. Also, wherever you go, don't forget a camera so you can take pictures!

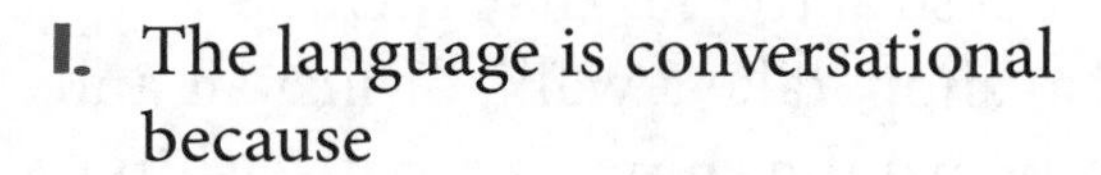

1. The language is conversational because

- Ⓐ there is a question in the text to engage the reader.
- Ⓑ a conversation occurs between two characters.
- Ⓒ the author speaks in the text.
- Ⓓ the text is nonfiction.

2. Sunscreen and outdoors are _____.

- Ⓐ synonyms
- Ⓑ compound words
- Ⓒ antonyms
- Ⓓ homophones

3. According to the text, what should you bring no matter where you go?

____

____

4. How could you find out what the weather is like?

____

____

Name: ______________________________ Date: ______________

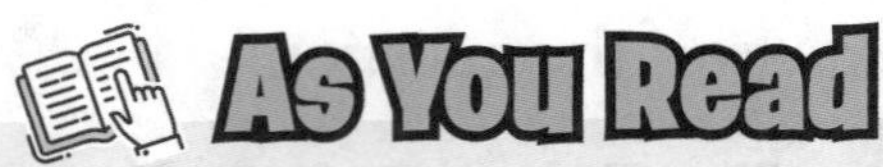

Look for and underline examples of compare and contrast in the text.

Welcome Aboard!

Welcome aboard! You are going on a cruise! A cruise is a special kind of vacation on a very large ship. Cruise ships travel to many different places. When people go on a cruise, they sleep in special rooms called cabins. Cabins are not very big, but they have beds and bathrooms. Most people don't spend very much time in their cabins, though. That is because there is so much to do on a cruise.

Different cruises last for different amounts of time. Some cruises last four days. Other cruises last as long as two weeks. During a cruise, the ship stops at different locations. People can get off the ship and visit those places while the ship is there. While people are visiting a location, they can do a variety of activities. These activities may include swimming, hiking, or exploring. They can also shop, take a walk, or just sit and relax. After several hours, people get back on board the ship. The cruise ship starts sailing toward the next location.

There are a lot of activities for people to do on cruise ships, too. Most cruise ships have pools for people to go swimming. Many cruise ships have games and contests to enter. Cruise ships also have plays, shows, and other fun activities for people. Some cruise ships offer miniature golf and tennis. Some cruise ships even offer rock climbing! Also, it's impossible to go hungry on a cruise ship. Each ship has a few restaurants and other dining rooms where people can eat. No matter what kind of food a person likes, they'll find it on a cruise ship.

Many people work on cruise ships to help keep people safe and make sure they have a good time. The captain is in charge of the ship. The cruise director is the person who organizes the activities. There are many other crew members, too. All crew members are there to answer questions, make sure the ship is safe, and make sure people are enjoying their cruise.

Name: ______________________ Date: ____________

Directions: Read "Welcome Aboard!" Then, answer the questions.

1. Does the title provide enough information to make a prediction about the text?
   - (A) Yes. It tells the reader that the text is about being aboard a train.
   - (B) Yes. It tells the reader that the text is about being aboard cruise ships.
   - (C) No. The text could be about being aboard a train, a ship, or an airplane.
   - (D) No. The text could be about being bored in the car.

2. Which sentence is true?
   - (A) All cruises last for one week.
   - (B) Most cruises have one restaurant.
   - (C) Cruises have many games, shows, and activities.
   - (D) The cruise director is in charge of the cruise ship.

3. A reader would most likely read the text to _____.
   - (A) find out what a cruise is like
   - (B) learn how to play tennis
   - (C) find out where to go swimming
   - (D) learn how to become a captain

4. Which is **not** something people can do on a cruise ship?
   - (A) shop
   - (B) play tennis
   - (C) swim
   - (D) hike

5. Compare different activities you could do when a cruise ship stops at a place.

Staying On the Cruise Ship	Getting off the Cruise Ship

Unit 6
WEEK 1
DAY
5

Name: ______________________ Date: ______________

Directions: Reread "Welcome Aboard!" Then, respond to the prompt.

Imagine you are on a cruise. Send a postcard to a friend or family member at home. Describe different activities you participated in. Use the text and your imagination. Then, draw and color a picture on the front of the postcard.

Name: ______________________ Date: ____________

Directions: Read the text, and answer the questions.

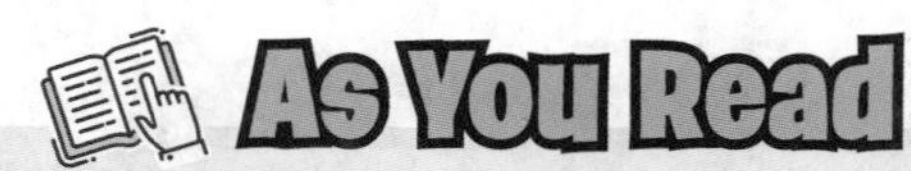

Underline one cause in the text and circle its effect.

Lost and Found

Cara and her parents sat down to discuss their upcoming summer vacation. Every year, Cara's family went to the beach. They rented a bungalow for two weeks. They would lay on the sand, swim in the ocean, and eat lots of ice cream.

"Let's vote on where to go this summer," Cara's dad said.

"I vote we go back to the beach!" Cara said.

"But last summer, it rained for five days straight," Cara's mom said. "You spent most of the time indoors playing video games. What if it rains again?"

Then her dad said, "Let's do something different. How about camping?"

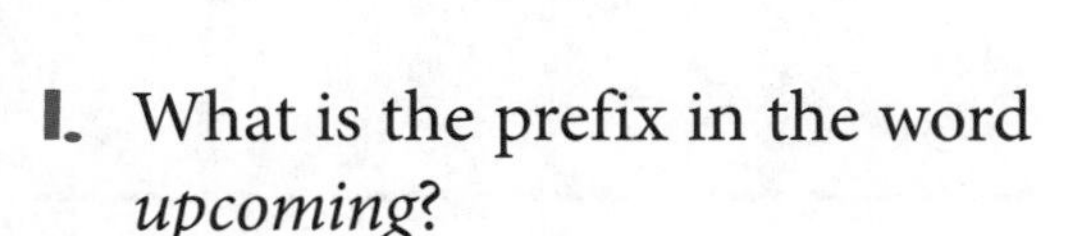

Cara's mouth fell open. "No way," she said.

But her parents outvoted her two to one. It was settled. They would spend their vacation in the woods.

1. What is the prefix in the word *upcoming*?

- (A) *–ing*
- (B) *up–*
- (C) *com–*
- (D) *–ming*

2. What causes Cara's parents to want to go camping?

- (A) Her mom wants the family to do something healthier.
- (B) Last year they ate too much ice cream.
- (C) Cara is tired of the beach.
- (D) Last year it rained for five days.

3. What is the meaning of *straight* in this text?

- (A) curvy
- (B) boring
- (C) in a row
- (D) not bending

4. How many syllables are in the word *outvoted*?

- (A) three
- (B) one
- (C) two
- (D) four

Name: ______________________ Date: ______________

Directions: Read the text, and answer the questions.

Underline one cause in the text and circle its effect.

Going Camping

"This trip is going to be a monumental bore," Cara told her friends. "And worse, there's undoubtedly zero cell reception in the woods."

Plus, the last time Cara had been to the woods, she had been eaten alive by mosquitoes. So, she tried telling her parents that after school.

"Can't we camp in the backyard and then go to the beach?" asked Cara.

Ignoring her, her parents concentrated on a map spread out on a table.

"Wouldn't it be easier to use the maps app on your phone?" asked Cara.

"We're doing this vacation old school," her dad said.

"Let's go to Lakeland State Park," said her mom. "It has forests, rivers, and plenty of hiking trails."

"Does it have a hotel we can retreat to every night?" Cara asked.

Her father laughed and shook his head. "We're going to camp out in a tent, and it will be so fun!"

"Oh, no!" moaned Cara.

1. What is the root word in *undoubtedly*?
   - (A) *un–*
   - (B) doubted
   - (C) doubt
   - (D) *–ly*

2. What does the phrase *old school* mean?
   - (A) learning for teenagers
   - (B) using technology
   - (C) the easy way
   - (D) traditional

3. Why doesn't Cara want to go camping?
   - (A) She thinks they will get lost.
   - (B) She is worried it will rain.
   - (C) She is scared of staying in a motel.
   - (D) She thinks it will be boring.

4. Which is a synonym for *retreat*?
   - (A) withdraw
   - (B) hide
   - (C) attack
   - (D) shelter

Name: ______________________________ Date: ________________

Directions: Read the text, and answer the questions.

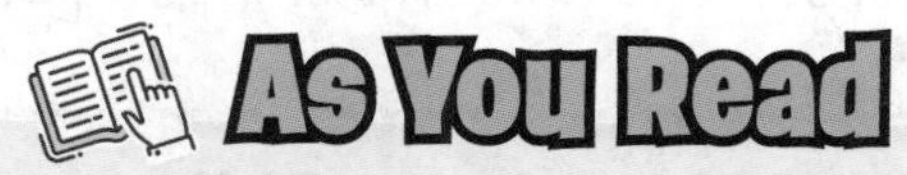

Underline one cause in the text and circle its effect.

Setting Up Camp

Cara's dad parked at their campsite, which was a large plot of dirt and grass, and started to unload their gear from the car. Cara tried to help set up the tent.

"This tent didn't come with instructions," she complained. "And FYI, the bug spray isn't working. The mosquitoes are having a royal feast!"

That evening, her dad cooked hot dogs on the campsite's grill.

"Don't leave extra food around, it'll attract bears," he warned.

"Bears!" Cara exclaimed. She ate her hot dog extra carefully, trying not to drop any crumbs.

There were more rules to follow: always carry water and don't drink from potentially contaminated streams were at the top of the list. The last two rules were to not eat any berries, and be on the lookout for bears when hiking.

"This trip is one big hazard," Cara said.

Her dad taught her how to use a pocket compass.

"Remember, our camp is due south of all hiking paths," he said.

Cara muttered, "It's like I'm stuck on some dangerous reality show."

1. Which word is a compound word?

- (A) outdoor
- (B) hot dogs
- (C) carrying
- (D) instructions

2. Cara compares the trip to ______.

- (A) a nightmare
- (B) a joke
- (C) a reality show
- (D) a nature show

3. Why are there rules when camping? Give a specific example from the text.

____

____

____

Name: ______________________________ Date: ________________

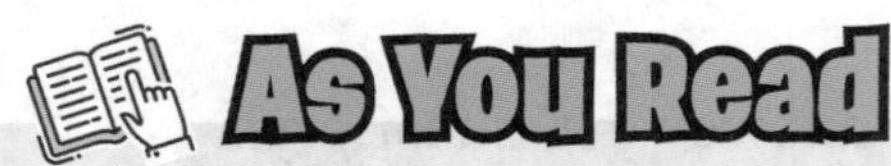

Underline two causes in the text and circle the effects of each.

An Amazing Hike

They next day, Cara and her parents followed a trail through a deep forest. It was an easy hike.

"That wasn't so bad," her mom said to Cara after they returned to the camp for lunch, and Cara nodded to be agreeable.

After eating, Cara decided to take a short walk by herself on a different trail. Soon, she heard the sound of a waterfall and went off trail to have a look. The sight of all that water made her thirsty, but she had forgotten to bring her bottle. She was about to drink some of the water from the falls when she remembered her father's warning. The water could be full of germs!

I'd better get back, she thought, but she slipped on some wet stones and twisted her ankle. Hobbling in pain, she took the wrong path back to the trail. Now she didn't know where she was! She tried to retrace her steps, but after an hour, she had only managed to work up an appetite.

The berries on this bush look tasty, she thought, grabbing a handful. But then she remembered that her dad said they could be poisonous. Rain began falling, and with no shelter, Cara quickly got soaked.

Then, she remembered the pocket compass. The campsite was due south. Using the compass to guide her, she walked through the trees, sometimes tripping. Suddenly, she saw a dark figure in the distance. It was a bear!

Cara ducked behind a fallen log. She peeked above the log to watch the bear. It was wandering around yet hadn't spotted her. She started to relax. Eventually, the bear walked in another direction. Cara couldn't believe it. Seeing an amazing animal in the wild, not in a zoo, was awesome!

As Cara went back to walking, she began to notice beautiful flowers, cute chipmunks, and so many birds. Soon, she met the original trail and followed it back to camp. She had survived! Her parents were so relieved to see her.

That night, Cara felt good. Her day had been a bit scary, but also exciting. It was as if she had been in a video game instead of watching one on a screen.

"I guess you were right—this trip was a hazard," said her father. "You probably want to hit a beach next summer."

Cara smiled and said, "Not necessarily!"

Name: ______________________ **Date:** ______________

Directions: Read "An Amazing Hike." Then, answer the questions.

1. What does the suffix *re–* mean in *retrace*?

- (A) to do it again
- (B) to do it differently
- (C) to not do it
- (D) to do it faster

2. Why does Cara duck behind a fallen log?

- (A) She feels hungry and thirsty.
- (B) She sees a bear in the forest.
- (C) Her ankle is hurting.
- (D) She is trying to figure out how to use the compass.

3. What part of speech is the word *cute*?

- (A) noun
- (B) verb
- (C) adjective
- (D) pronoun

4. What hint is given in the last sentence of the story?

- (A) Cara is beginning to like camping.
- (B) Cara can't wait to go to the beach next summer.
- (C) Cara's dad thinks camping is too dangerous.
- (D) Cara's dad is proud of her for hiking.

5. Write two examples of cause and effect from the story.

Cause	Effect

Name: ______________________________ Date: ____________

Directions: Reread "An Amazing Hike." Then, respond to the prompt.

Cara thought she would hate camping, but she ends up liking it. Think about something you thought you wouldn't like but ended up changing your mind about. It might be a sport, an activity, a food, a movie, or a book. Write a story about the experience. Be sure to describe what happened to make you change your mind. Your writing should have a beginning, middle, and end.

Name: ______________________ Date: ______________

Arizona's Grand Canyon, a wonder of the world

Dear Ellen,

It's been an amazing road trip so far! We finally reached the Grand Canyon, and it was worth the long ride. I stepped onto a skywalk that sticks out over the canyon. It's a glass walkway that makes you feel like you're going to fall all the way to the bottom! On our way out west, we saw the Rock and Roll Hall of Fame in Cleveland, Wrigley Field in Chicago, and the Gateway Arch in St. Louis. Dad insisted we stop in Kansas to see the world's biggest ball of twine. My brother is actually behaving for once in the back seat (he hasn't kicked me once) and Mom and Dad are listening to CDs of some band they like called the Eagles. They're pretty cool! Our next stops are San Diego and La Jolla Beach. I can't wait to hit the Pacific Ocean. Wish you were here!

Your friend,
Cindy

Cindy Benson
902 E. 88th St.
New York, NY 10128

Name: ______________________________ Date: ________________

Directions: Read the postcard. Then, answer the questions.

1. Which word is an antonym of *amazing*?
   - (A) awesome
   - (B) ordinary
   - (C) great
   - (D) funny

2. Where is Cindy going next?
   - (A) Kansas
   - (B) San Diego
   - (C) Chicago
   - (D) Los Angeles

3. How should *insisted* be broken into syllables?
   - (A) in·sist·ed
   - (B) in·sis·ted
   - (C) insist·ed
   - (D) ins·ist·ed

4. How does Cindy seem to feel about her vacation?
   - (A) hopeful
   - (B) bored
   - (C) homesick
   - (D) excited

5. Complete the web with sights and cities Cindy saw during her travels.

Road Trip Stops

Name: ______________________________ **Date:** ________________

Directions: Closely read these texts. Study the postcard on page 113. Look for different types of vacation activities mentioned. Record them in the table.

Close-Reading Texts

Vacation Variety	Going Camping
There are many different kinds of vacations and even more things to do on vacation. Some people like to be outdoors. Hiking and camping are good vacations for these people. Other people like to go swimming. They like warm weather and sandy beaches. People who like sun, sand, and the perfect place to swim often go to the ocean. Some people prefer big cities. They like to visit museums and go to restaurants.	"Can't we camp in the backyard and then go to the beach?" asked Cara. Ignoring her, her parents concentrated on a map spread out on a table. "Wouldn't it be easier to use the maps app on your phone?" asked Cara. "We're doing this vacation old school," her dad said. "Let's go to Lakeland State Park," said her mom. "It has forests, rivers, and plenty of hiking trails."

Vacation Variety	Going Camping	Postcard

Name: ______________________________ Date: ______________

Directions: Closely read these texts. Write two sentences describing how they are different and one sentence describing how they are the same.

Close-Reading Texts

The Importance of Vacations	An Amazing Hike
But did you know that vacations are good for you? It's true! Vacations allow you to rest, and rest is very important because it keeps you healthy. Rest supports your body and your mind by helping you think better and improving your mood. Vacations provide much more than just rest, though. They also allow you to jump, run, swim, and play. Being active is very good for you. When you move your body, you help your body stay healthy.	Cara ducked behind a fallen log. She peeked above the log to watch the bear. It was wandering around yet hadn't spotted her. She started to relax. Eventually, the bear walked in another direction. Cara couldn't believe it. Seeing an amazing animal in the wild, not in a zoo, was awesome! As Cara went back to walking, she began to notice beautiful flowers, cute chipmunks, and so many birds.

Different

____

____

____

____

Same

____

____

____

____

Name: ______________________________ Date: ______________

Directions: Reread the postcard on page 113. Then, respond to the prompt.

Think of somewhere you would love to travel. Write a paragraph to convince your family to plan a trip there. Your paragraph should have introduction and conclusion sentences. It should also give at least three reasons why your location would be a good place to visit.

Name: ______________________________ Date: ________________

Directions: Think of a fun place you have been in your community. Send a postcard to a friend, and describe where you went and what you did. Then, draw a picture to go on the front of your postcard.

Name: ______________________ Date: ______________

Directions: Read the text, and answer the questions.

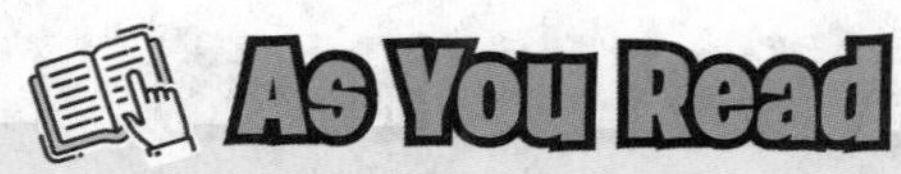

Draw a star next to information that you find interesting or surprising.

Bow and Arrow History

Bows and arrows have a very long history. Long ago, people made the first arrows from wood. They burned wood and then sharpened it into points. Later, people made arrows with sharpened stone tips.

Bows and arrows made it much easier for people to hunt. Before these tools were invented, hunters had to use sharpened sticks or spears. But a hunter had to get very close to a wild animal to use a stick or spear. This made hunting pretty dangerous. Bows and arrows were much safer hunting tools. They let hunters keep a safe distance away from their prey.

Bows and arrows are used today. Some people may use them when they go hunting. Other people like to use them as a hobby. They shoot arrows at targets and hope to hit the bull's-eye in the center. An arrow whistling through the air is a beautiful thing to watch!

1. Why was it dangerous to hunt with spears?

- (A) Spears could be thrown from far away.
- (B) Spears were faster than the animals.
- (C) Spears were loud and alerted prey.
- (D) Hunters sometimes needed to get close to wild animals.

2. Which is a synonym for *dangerous*?

- (A) secure
- (B) risky
- (C) enormous
- (D) nervous

3. Which shows the correct pronunciation of *sharpened*?

- (A) shahr-PUHN-ed
- (B) shahr-PUHND
- (C) SHAHR-puhn-ed
- (D) SHAHR-puhn-D

4. *An arrow whistles through the air!* The word *whistles* tells ______.

- (A) the size of the arrow
- (B) the color of the arrow
- (C) the speed of the arrow
- (D) the noise the arrow makes

Name: ______________________ Date: ______________

Directions: Read the text, and answer the questions.

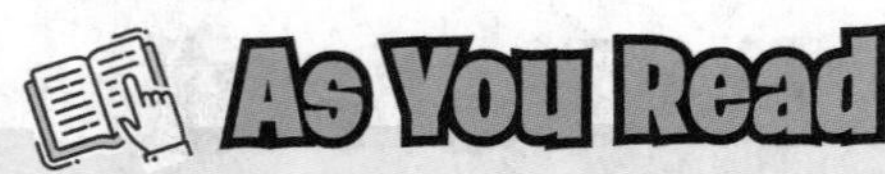

Draw a star next to information that you find interesting or surprising.

Parts of an Arrow

Arrows might look very simple, but they are made of several parts that all work together. The arrowhead is the sharpened point of an arrow. This part hits the target or the prey. The arrowhead is connected to the shaft. The shaft is the long, straight part of an arrow. Along the shaft is called fletching. Fletching is the group of plastic feathers on an arrow. Fletching is what gives an arrow balance. It helps an arrow move in a straight line. At the very end of the shaft is the nock. This is a little plastic slot that is used to fit an arrow into the string of a bow.

Arrows can be made of different materials. Some arrows are made of wood. But many are made of aluminum (uh-LOO-muh-nuhm). Aluminum is the same metal used to make cans. Regardless of what material is used to make arrows, they all have the same parts.

1. What would best help clarify the parts of an arrow described in this text?

- (A) a labeled diagram of an arrow
- (B) a thesaurus
- (C) a friend who likes to read
- (D) a glossary definition

2. Which can be used to find the meaning of the word *fletching*?

- (A) the internet
- (B) a glossary
- (C) a dictionary
- (D) all of the above

3. Which is a synonym for *connected*?

- (A) apart
- (B) joined
- (C) next to
- (D) larger

4. Which syllable is stressed in the word *aluminum*?

- (A) the first syllable
- (B) the second syllable
- (C) the third syllable
- (D) the fourth syllable

Name: ______________________________ Date: ________________

Directions: Read the text, and answer the questions.

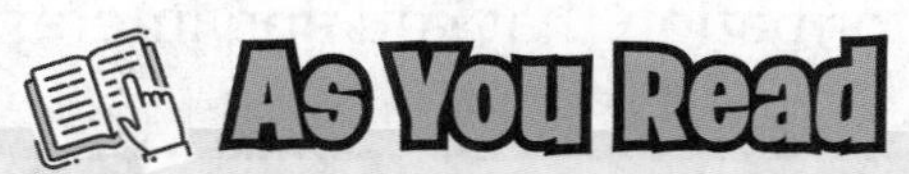

Draw a star next to information that you find interesting or surprising.

An Arrow's Flight

There are several steps to shooting an arrow. First, you fit the arrow onto the string of the bow. Then, you draw the string back toward you. When you do this, you are storing energy that will be used to move the arrow through the air. Finally, you release the string, which sends the arrow flying.

When you shoot an arrow, it doesn't fly perfectly straight. An arrow actually flies in an arch pattern, which is why people who shoot arrows are called archers. When you first shoot an arrow, it goes up because of the force you used to shoot. But gravity pulls it back down. If you use enough force, the arrow will hit the target before it hits the ground. If you land your arrow in the center of the target, you get a bull's-eye!

1. In this text, what does *draw* mean?
   - (A) sketch
   - (B) an even score
   - (C) pull
   - (D) lengthen

2. Which word has the same root word as *archers*?
   - (A) parched
   - (B) arrow
   - (C) ranch
   - (D) archery

3. How did archers get their name?

   ____

   ____

4. What types of physical skills would a person need to be a skilled archer?

   ____

   ____

Name: ____________________ Date: ____________

Draw a star next to information that you find interesting or surprising.

Bull's-Eye!

Have you ever wondered what it would be like to use a bow and arrow? People have used bows and arrows for thousands of years, and many people use them today. Archery, the skill of shooting with a bow and arrow, is a very popular sport. It is even an Olympic event! People love to see their arrows hit the bull's-eye at the center of a target. Archery is a fairly safe sport, but the fact that it requires the use of sharp, flying objects might make you think otherwise. It is actually safer than contact sports, such as baseball and football.

Archery requires both physical and mental skill. When you shoot arrows, you use your upper body. Using your body in this way helps to keep it strong. Shooting arrows also helps you mentally. This is because you must keep your mind focused on what you are doing and the target. You must block out other things. Practicing staying focused helps you think better.

Almost anyone can learn archery. You can easily start as a beginner. You do not have to be very big or strong. You do not have to buy expensive bows and arrows. You can rent bows and arrows from an archery club. Many clubs offer lessons so you can learn from an experienced archer. You can take private lessons or lessons with other kids. You may even make some new friends!

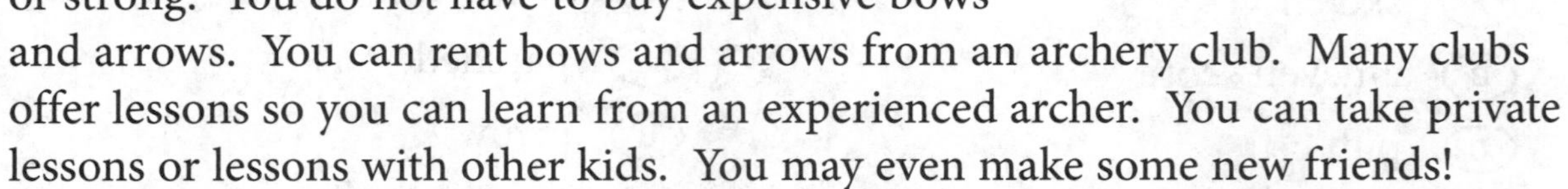

Archery is a safe and fun sport, but you still need to be careful. Make sure to take lessons from an expert. Having an adult with you when you are practicing is key. It is also important to shoot arrows in a safe place. Most archery clubs have safe places for practicing. They have safety measures in place so you can practice there without hurting anyone. When you are at a club, make sure to follow all the rules. They are there to keep you safe. It is also important to use safe equipment. Keeping your bows and arrows in good shape is important. If you do it safely, archery can be a lot of fun. So be safe, have fun, and hit that bull's-eye!

Name: ______________________________ Date: ______________

Directions: Read "Bull's-Eye!" Then, answer the questions.

1. Based on the title alone, a reader might think this is about _____.

- (A) target shooting
- (B) archery
- (C) darts
- (D) all of the above

2. The author probably wrote this to _____.

- (A) warn of how incredibly dangerous archery can be
- (B) introduce a fun sport
- (C) help get an archery business going
- (D) all of the above

3. Which is **not** true about archery?

- (A) It helps you focus.
- (B) There are no rules.
- (C) Anyone can learn it.
- (D) It is an Olympic event.

4. Which is the best summary of this text?

- (A) Archery is a safe sport. It is safer than sports that use balls.
- (B) People like archery because they love to see their arrows hit the bull's-eye.
- (C) If you are careful, archery is a fun and safe sport that is also good for you.
- (D) Archery clubs have safe places to practice shooting.

5. Write the main idea for each paragraph. Use your own words.

Paragraph 1	
Paragraph 2	
Paragraph 3	
Paragraph 4	

Name: ______________________ **Date:** ______________

Directions: Reread "Bull's-Eye!" Then, respond to the prompt.

Many people enjoy archery. Think of a sport, hobby, or activity you enjoy. Write a paragraph comparing it to archery. Describe how they are similar and different. Don't forget an introduction and a conclusion sentence.

Name: ______________________ Date: ______________

Directions: Read the text, and answer the questions.

Make notes of connections you find between this text and another you've read.

Taking Aim

Sophia couldn't wait for school to be over so she could keep reading a book she had gotten from the library. It was a story about Robin Hood. He was a famous outlaw from long ago who robbed from the rich to give to the poor. Robin was a skilled archer. One picture in the book showed Robin with his bow and arrow. It reminded Sophia of one of her favorite characters, Katniss. She was the hero of The Hunger Games books. She shot arrows with a bow.

Sophia wondered if people still used bows and arrows. At home, she searched the internet. She found that archery was an Olympic sport. Sophia loved to play team sports, especially basketball. She liked soccer, too. But archery was a sport for individuals. She was intrigued by that idea.

1. How does Sophia get interested in archery?
   - Ⓐ the Olympics
   - Ⓑ Robin Hood
   - Ⓒ team sports
   - Ⓓ the internet

2. What intrigues Sophia about archery?
   - Ⓐ It uses a bow and arrow.
   - Ⓑ It is a team sport.
   - Ⓒ It was played long ago.
   - Ⓓ It is in books she has read.

3. How many syllables are in the word *individuals*?
   - Ⓐ two
   - Ⓑ five
   - Ⓒ four
   - Ⓓ six

4. How are the characters Robin Hood and Katniss similar?
   - Ⓐ They both shoot bows and arrows.
   - Ⓑ They both steal from the rich.
   - Ⓒ They were both in the Olympics.
   - Ⓓ They both like soccer.

Name: ________________________________ Date: ________________

Directions: Read the text, and answer the questions.

Make notes of connections you find between this text and another you've read.

Getting Started

Sophia found a place in her neighborhood that taught archery lessons. But she didn't want to go by herself. So, she called her friend Rory and told him all about it.

"Want to sign up with me?" she asked.

"Sounds like fun," he said.

After school, Sophia and Rory walked to The Archery Shoppe. In the store, all types of bows, arrows, strings, and other equipment lined the shelves. The store's instructor showed Sophia and Rory around, and he explained the equipment, too.

"The fanciest bows we have are compound bows and recurve bows," the instructor said. "They're for experts."

Sophia blushed and said, "The only arrow I ever shot had a rubber suction tip."

The instructor smiled. "No problem! Most people don't even have any experience. Let's start with a traditional bow."

"This is like the kind Katniss and Robin Hood used," Sophia told Rory.

"Amazing," Rory grinned. "I can't wait for us to get some bull's-eyes."

1. How should *rubber* be divided into syllables?
   - (A) rubb·er
   - (B) ru·bber
   - (C) ru·bb·er
   - (D) rub·ber

2. Which type of bow does the instructor give Sophia?
   - (A) suction cup
   - (B) traditional
   - (C) compound
   - (D) recurve

3. Which word is a synonym of *fanciest*?
   - (A) elaborate
   - (B) simple
   - (C) plain
   - (D) popular

4. Which shooting equipment is **not** mentioned at the store?
   - (A) string
   - (B) arrows
   - (C) gloves
   - (D) bows

Name: ______________________ Date: ______________

Directions: Read the text, and answer the questions.

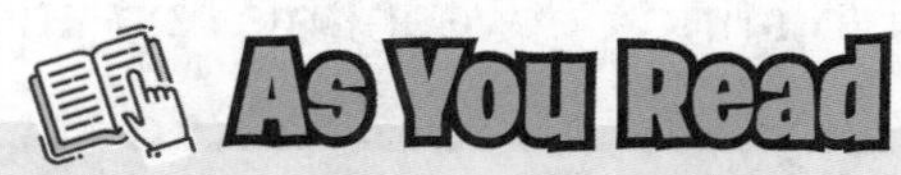

Make notes of connections you find between this text and another you've read.

Getting Competitive

Sophia was a long way from a bull's-eye. Her first shot was super embarrassing. She focused all her attention on the target and let go of the string. The arrow flew about halfway to the target. Then, it fell to the ground.

Rory's first arrow hit the outer edge of the target. He crowed, "Wow, I'm like a superhero!"

Sophia cheered for him. Secretly, she felt irritated that he was naturally good. Still, over the weeks, Sophia got better. She began to hit the inner circles of the target. Once, she even hit a bull's-eye! She had never felt prouder.

One day, the instructor told Sophia and Rory, "The shop is holding a competition. It's for kids in your age group."

"I'm going to win this easily," Rory boasted. "You're toast."

Sophia rolled her eyes, annoyed by his attitude. She was determined to do her best.

1. Why is Sophia embarrassed after her first shot?

Ⓐ Rory told her she was bad at archery.
Ⓑ The arrow didn't make it to the target.
Ⓒ Her arrow hit the bull's-eye.
Ⓓ She didn't hold her bow the right way.

2. What is a synonym of *crowed*?

Ⓐ bragged
Ⓑ said
Ⓒ whispered
Ⓓ strutted

3. How would you describe Rory? Use the text to support your answer.

____

____

4. What do you predict will happen next? Explain your thinking.

____

____

Name: ______________________ Date: ______________

Make notes of connections you find between this text and another you've read.

Who Is the Best Archer?

At the competition, the instructor explained the rules. There were 15 rounds. In each round, contestants shot three arrows at a target. The closer the arrow landed to the bull's-eye, the more points they earned.

Soon, it was Sophia's turn. Her first arrow earned only one point. Her next two arrows landed closer to the center.

"I didn't do so well," she told Rory.

He cackled, "I'm way ahead of you!"

The targets were moved back. Sophia's aim improved each round. But Rory wasn't doing as well as he hoped.

"There must be something wrong with the arrows or my bow," he muttered.

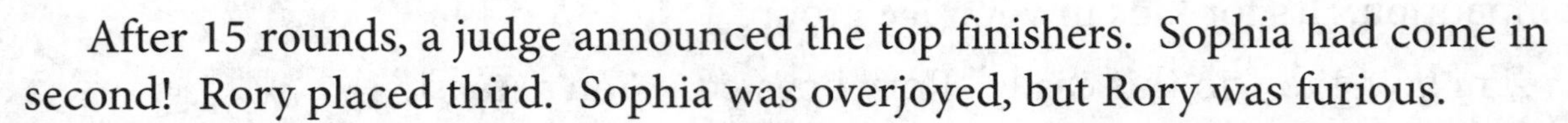

After 15 rounds, a judge announced the top finishers. Sophia had come in second! Rory placed third. Sophia was overjoyed, but Rory was furious.

"I can't believe I finished third," he said. "I'm definitely better than you."

Sophia's eyes went wide. "Rory, that was super rude."

Days later, Rory called Sophia.

"I wanted to say sorry," he told her. "I got upset because you beat me. Will you come practice with me at the park?"

"Thanks, Rory," said Sophia, "and sure, I'll meet you there."

Sophia had brought balloons for practice. She tied a couple to a tree. Rory hit more balloons than Sophia. He was gleeful when he outshot her.

"I told you I was a better archer," he taunted her.

Annoyed, Sophia replied, "But I still did better in the competition."

Rory sputtered, "I'll prove how good I am." He balanced a balloon on her head. Then, he aimed an arrow at her.

"Rory, no way!" Sophia cried. "Come on, we're friends."

Rory looked down. "I know. I guess I just hate losing. I'm sorry."

"Hey," said Sophia, "maybe you'll beat me in the next competition."

Rory laughed. "You're right! I can't wait, Ms. Robin Hood!"

Name: ______________________________ Date: ________________

Directions: Read "Who Is the Best Archer?" Then, answer the questions.

1. What is the past tense of *carry*?

- (A) carryed
- (B) carried
- (C) carries
- (D) carrys

2. What is a synonym of *overjoyed*?

- (A) happy
- (B) jealous
- (C) sad
- (D) calm

3. Which of these statements about the text is true?

- (A) Sophia has a strong start to the competition.
- (B) Rory improves as the tournament goes on.
- (C) Rory beats Sophia in the tournament.
- (D) Sophia comes in second place.

4. How does Rory feel after the tournament?

- (A) satisfied
- (B) proud
- (C) excited
- (D) angry

5. Write at least three words or phrases to describe Sophia and Rory.

Sophia	Rory

Name: ______________________________ **Date:** ______________

Directions: Reread "Who Is the Best Archer?" Then, respond to the prompt.

In this story, Sophia beats Rory in the tournament. What if their places were reversed so that Sophia finished third and Rory finished second? Write an alternate story ending. Tell what might have happened with this change.

Name: ____________________ Date: ____________

WELCOME TO ARROW ARCHERY!

Come visit us at 29 Sher Wood Rd!

Open Monday–Saturday, 10 a.m. to 9 p.m.

We are proud to announce our grand opening in our city's grandest neighborhood! Our store and range is housed in a renovated warehouse. Join us and take part in the oldest sport in history. Bows and arrows have been used by almost every civilization on Earth. Be part of the tradition!

Arrow Archery is great for both beginners and skilled archers. Our 30 sleek, modern archery lanes are state-of-the-art. They are sure to bring out the Robin Hood in you: We guarantee it!

Our shop carries the highest-end equipment. Choose from many types of bows, from simple to professional. We carry every kind of arrow. Pick wood, plastic or metal. It's your choice. You can buy or rent anything in our store!

Arrow Archery offers private instruction* from our brilliant staff. Many of our instructors have won gold medals in archery.

Arrow Archery has programs for kids. We have tournaments for all ages and levels of skill.**

If you're looking for a fun time, Arrow Archery is a definite bull's-eye!

*Classes begin at $35 an hour.

**Kids must be 10 years of age or older to take part in our program.

Name: ______________________ Date: ______________

Directions: Read "Welcome to Arrow Archery!" Then, answer the questions.

1. What type of text is "Welcome to Arrow Archery"?

- (A) magazine article
- (B) poem
- (C) advertisement
- (D) fiction story

2. What is the meaning of the word *programs* in the text?

- (A) series of instructions to control a computer
- (B) papers giving details about a performance
- (C) shows on television or radio
- (D) several planned events with a goal or purpose

3. Which statement is true?

- (A) Many of the instructors are gold medal winners.
- (B) Students must be at least 12 years old to take lessons.
- (C) The shop has only wood and metal arrows.
- (D) Lessons cost $25 an hour.

4. *Metal* and *medal* are ___.

- (A) homophones
- (B) synonyms
- (C) antonyms
- (D) contractions

5. Why might a person who loves history want to take archery lessons?

____

____

____

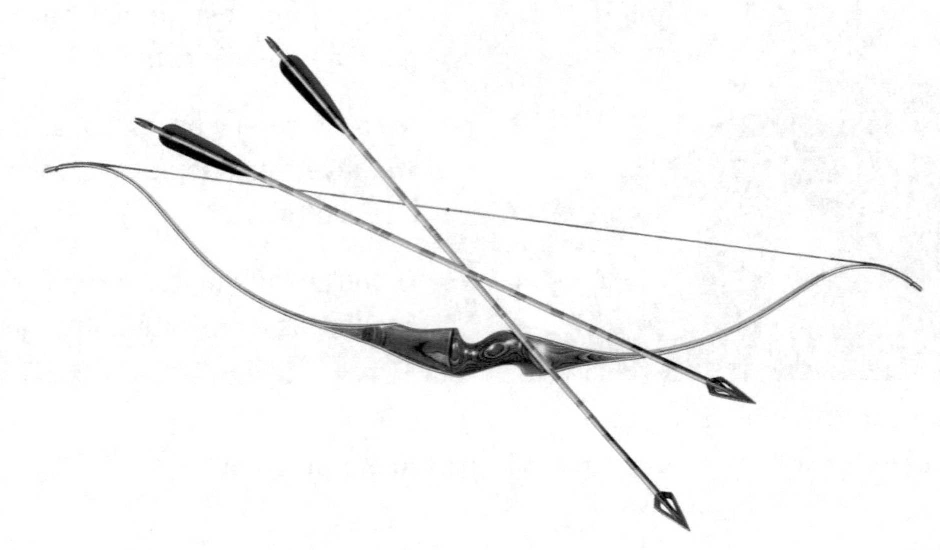

Name: ______________________ Date: ______________

Directions: Closely read these texts. Study the advertisement on page 131. Look for different materials bows and arrows can be made of and different uses. Record your findings in the table.

Close-Reading Texts

Bow and Arrow History	Getting Started
Long ago, people made the first arrows from wood. They burned wood and then sharpened it into points. Later, people made arrows with sharpened stone tips. Bows and arrows made it much easier for people to hunt.	In the store, all types of bows, arrows, strings, and other equipment lined the shelves. The store's instructor showed Sophia and Rory around, and he explained the equipment, too. "The fanciest bows we have are compound bows and recurve bows," the instructor said. "They're for experts." Sophia blushed and said, "The only arrow I ever shot had a rubber suction tip."

Bow and Arrow History	
Getting Started	
Welcome to Archery!	

Name: ______________________________ Date: ______________

Directions: Closely read these texts. Think about their genres, main ideas, and what you noticed in each. Then, compare and contrast the texts in the table.

Close-Reading Texts

An Arrow's Flight	Getting Competitive
When you shoot an arrow, it doesn't fly perfectly straight. An arrow actually flies in an arch pattern, which is why people who shoot arrows are called archers. When you first shoot an arrow, it goes up because of the force you used to shoot. But gravity pulls it back down. If you use enough force, the arrow will hit the target before it hits the ground. If you land your arrow in the center of the target, you get a bull's-eye!	Sophia was a long way from a bull's-eye. Her first shot was super embarrassing. She focused all her attention on the target and let go of the string. The arrow flew about halfway to the target. Then, it fell to the ground.

An Arrow's Flight	Getting Competitive
Both	

Name: ______________________ Date: ______________

Directions: Think about the text from this unit. Then, respond to the prompt.

Imagine a child saw the archery advertisement. They are interested in taking lessons. Write a conversation between the child and their parent to decide if they will try archery. Include information from the ad in the conversation.

Name: ______________________________ Date: ________________

Directions: Create an advertisement similar to the one on page 131. But, make it for a lesson you could give to another person. It might be about a sport, hobby, or talent. Include a description of the lesson, where and when it will be, and how much you will charge. Add pictures to tell more about the lesson.

Name: ______________________________ Date: ____________________

Directions: Read the text, and answer the questions.

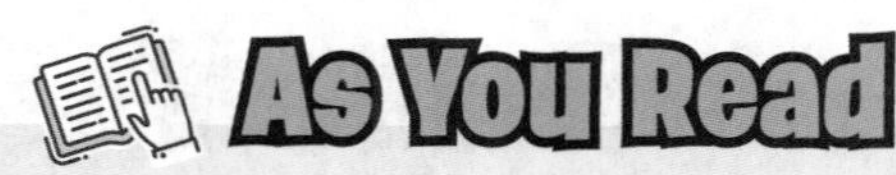

Write a quick note comparing modern times to an event in the text.

Fear and Understanding

As we learn more about our world, we understand it better. And when we learn more about something, we are often less afraid of it. For example, when cars were first invented, many people were afraid of them. They didn't want to ride in them. Safety was a big concern. But people have learned a lot about cars since then, and they now understand them better. So, most people have stopped being afraid of them. The same thing is true of electricity. In the early 1800s, many people were afraid of electricity. They didn't know how it worked. That made them fearful. Today, people know a lot about how electricity works, so most people are not afraid of it. If people use it safely, it won't hurt them. It goes to show that the more you know about things, the less scary they are!

1. The first two sentences indicate that the text is about _____.

- (A) fear and how the world is really large
- (B) fear and how it is unstoppable
- (C) fear and overcoming it through knowledge
- (D) fear and why parachuting is scary

2. Which is the root of *electricity*?

- (A) electrical
- (B) elec
- (C) electric
- (D) ele

3. Another word for *scary* is _____.

- (A) boiling
- (B) infuriating
- (C) boring
- (D) frightening

4. What is one point the author makes?

- (A) As we learn about things, we become less afraid of them.
- (B) As we discover electricity, we slowly drive our cars better.
- (C) People drove scary cars in the 1800s, but now they do not.
- (D) As we learn about things, we become more afraid of them.

Name: ______________________ Date: ______________

Directions: Read the text, and answer the questions.

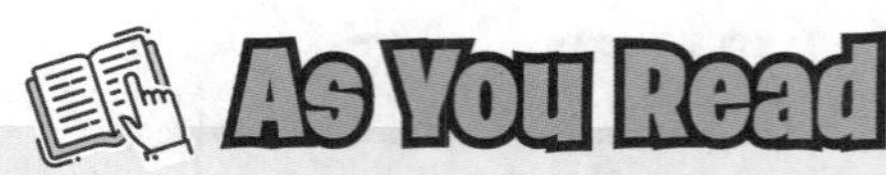

Write a quick note comparing modern times to an event in the text.

Life in the 1800s

Life was very different in the early 1800s compared to today. For example, people did not have automobiles or trains. They rode on horses or used carriages. People did not have electricity either. Most people used candles for light. They had fireplaces for heat. The invention of the steam engine was a huge change. This engine allowed machines to make things faster and easier. Steam engines were used in factories.

At this time, life was good for people who were very, very rich. But most people were not wealthy. In fact, over half of England's people were poor. Life was very hard for them. Many poor people worked in factories. A lot of children also worked in factories instead of going to school. And the factories were not safe. Many people who worked in factories got hurt. Other people got sick from chemicals they worked with. Some people even died.

1. In what way was life different in the 1800s?

- (A) Some people were rich.
- (B) Children worked in factories.
- (C) They had electric lights.
- (D) Trains were used for transportation.

2. The root word in *wealthy* is _____.

- (A) weal
- (B) we
- (C) wealth
- (D) healthy

3. A synonym for *automobile* is _____.

- (A) engine
- (B) mobile
- (C) train
- (D) car

4. To create exaggeration, which phrase could replace *very, very rich*?

- (A) infinitely rich
- (B) somewhat rich
- (C) rich, but only a little
- (D) not very rich

Name: ______________________________ Date: ______________

Directions: Read the text, and answer the questions.

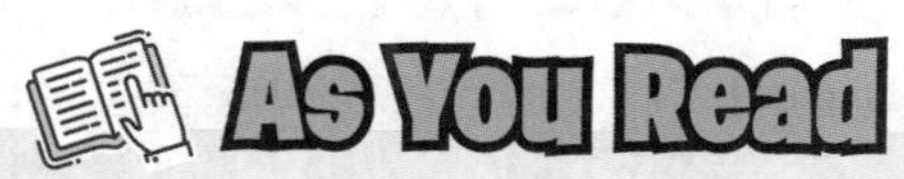

Write a quick note comparing modern times to an event in the text.

Fear of Change

In the early 1800s, life was changing very fast. Many people moved from farms to cities. People started to work in factories. Some people didn't like the big changes. They saw that there was a lot of sickness, pollution, and poverty. They thought life was becoming too dangerous and stressful. These people thought that humans had gone too far with technology. They were afraid of what would happen if more machines were created.

One woman wrote a book about this idea. Her name was Mary Shelley. Her book was called *Frankenstein* (FRANG-kuhn-styn). The book is about a man who makes a new creature. But when he sees what he has done, he realizes he has gone too far. This book became very popular. It is sometimes called the first science-fiction novel.

1. Which literary genre is *Frankenstein*?
   - (A) nonfiction
   - (B) science fiction
   - (C) realistic fiction
   - (D) fairy tale

2. A novel is a kind of ______.
   - (A) recipe
   - (B) book
   - (C) machine
   - (D) dictionary

3. Why were people upset about the big changes happening?

____

____

4. Why do you think *Frankenstein* was such a popular book?

____

____

Name: ______________________ Date: ______________

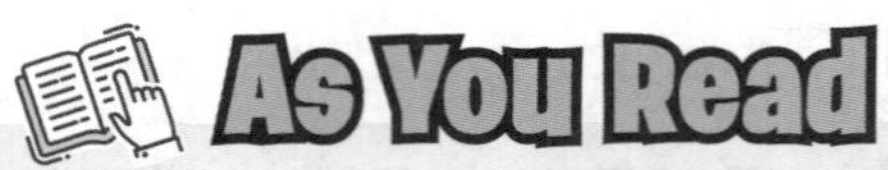

Write a quick note comparing modern times to an event in the text.

Mary Shelley's Life

Mary Shelley was born on August 30, 1797. Her mother died soon after she was born, so Mary was raised by her father. Four years later, William married again. William's new wife had children of her own. So, Mary grew up with four brothers and sisters.

Mary grew up in an unusual way. At the time, girls did not usually go to school. But her father thought that girls should learn just as much as boys did. Her father was friends with many great scientists, poets, and writers. So, Mary grew up reading lots of books and poems. She was surrounded by ideas. She got a good education.

One of her father's friends was a poet. His name was Percy Shelley. Percy and Mary became friends and then fell in love. They got married when Mary was 16.

In the summer of 1816, Mary and Percy took a trip with some friends. The weather was bad, so the group had to stay inside. One day, they decided to see who could write the best scary story. Mary's idea for a story came to her in a dream. She would write a story about a man who wanted to create a new creature. But when he saw what he made, he realized he had gone too far. Mary shared her story with the group. It was very scary. Everyone agreed that Mary's story was the best scary story.

Two years later, that story was made into a book called *Frankenstein*. The book became popular right away. At 18, Mary Shelley was a famous writer! Her book made people think a lot. It was also a good scary story.

Mary continued to write for the rest of her life. She published more books. She had two children named Clara and William. After a few years, her family moved to Italy. There, Percy became a very famous poet. Sadly, Percy died in Italy. Mary went back to England with her children. She died there in 1851.

Name: ______________________________ Date: ________________

Directions: Read "Mary Shelley's Life." Then, answer the questions.

1. Based on the first sentence, the reader can tell this text is _____.
   - (A) autobiographical in nature
   - (B) biographical in nature
   - (C) science fiction
   - (D) a scientific text on deserts

2. Mary wrote *Frankenstein* because _____.
   - (A) she and her friends wanted to see who could write the best scary story
   - (B) she wanted to make her father happy
   - (C) she had many dreams and wanted to write about them
   - (D) she wanted to make a new kind of creature, but realized she went too far

3. Which do you think helped Mary to become a writer?
   - (A) Her family went to Italy.
   - (B) Her father thought that girls should learn just as much as boys.
   - (C) She enjoyed traveling with friends.
   - (D) Mary had two children named Clara and William.

4. What is the purpose for reading this text?
   - (A) to learn biographical information of Mary Shelley
   - (B) to learn about the character of Frankenstein
   - (C) for entertainment
   - (D) for entertainment and to learn about Percy Shelley

5. Choose three events from the story and add them to the time line. Write the year below the line and the event above it.

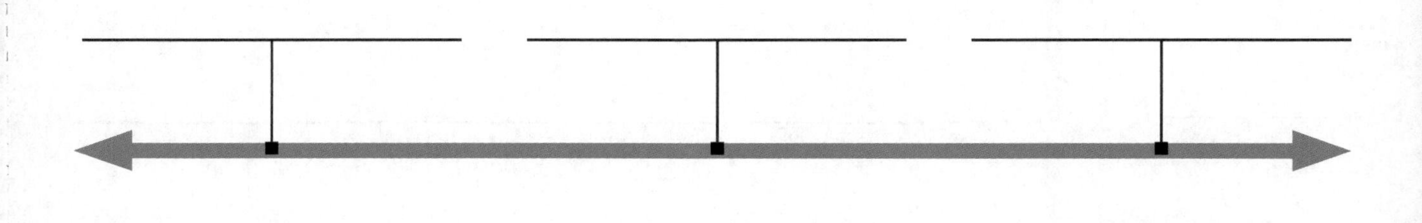

Name: ______________________ Date: ______________

Directions: Reread "Mary Shelley's Life." Then, respond to the prompt.

Mary Shelley had many important events in her life. So do you! Create a time line with seven events from your life so far. Your time line could include things such as being born, starting school, taking a trip, or beginning a sport. Include the year and a description for each event.

Name: ______________________ Date: ______________

Directions: Read the text, and answer the questions.

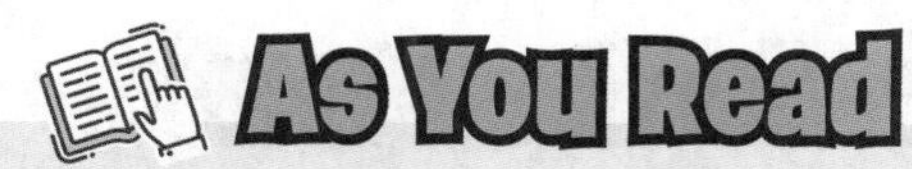

Circle words that describe the characters' actions.

My Favorite Monster

Max loved Friday nights. He always invited his friends from high school over to watch a movie. They sprawled out on the living room furniture, ate popcorn, and talked and laughed. Tonight, he and his friends watched a new horror movie.

"What's the scariest movie you've ever seen?" asked Max.

Ella said, "I like the classics. My favorite is *Halloween*—the original of course."

Lucas said, "*Jaws* is one I still have nightmares about. That shark was scary!"

Alexa frowned. "Ugh, definitely the movie with the clown!"

Max said, "The most frightening movie I've ever seen is *Frankenstein*."

"No way," Lucas scoffed. "That ancient black and white movie?"

"Yeah, man!" Max said. "Old horror movies are super great. I also like *Dracula* and *The Wolf Man*, but *Frankenstein* was the best for sure."

Max's friends were skeptical until he played it for them. When it ended, no one was laughing. Instead, they were mesmerized by what they had just seen.

1. What is the root word of *frightening*?
   - (A) frighten
   - (B) *–en*
   - (C) *–ing*
   - (D) fright

2. Why don't Max's friends want to watch Frankenstein at first?
   - (A) They think it is too old.
   - (B) They know it will be too scary.
   - (C) They are tired of movies.
   - (D) They have already seen it.

3. Which movie is **not** mentioned?
   - (A) *Halloween*
   - (B) *Creature From the Black Lagoon*
   - (C) *Jaws*
   - (D) *Dracula*

4. What is the meaning of *scoffed*?
   - (A) to laugh with understanding
   - (B) to react with anger
   - (C) to laugh with disapproval
   - (D) to react with humor

Name: ______________________________ Date: ________________

Directions: Read the text, and answer the questions.

Circle words that describe the characters' actions.

The Return of Frankenstein

The next day, Max could not get *Frankenstein* out of his head. He decided to read the novel that the movie was based on. It wasn't what he expected. First, the monster in the book could talk normally and was smart. The monster was chased to the North Pole. But he was frightening looking and did a lot of seriously bad things.

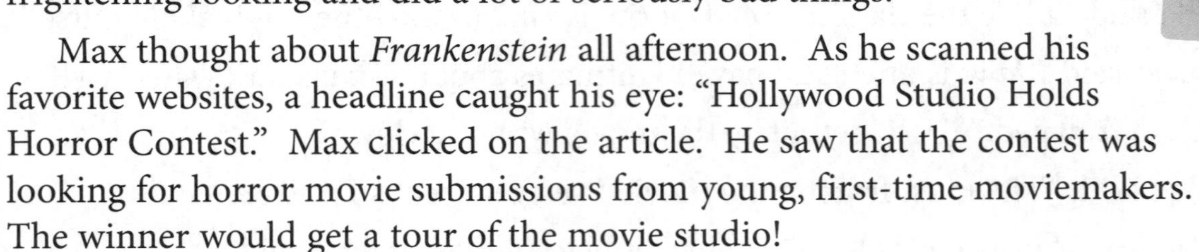

Max thought about *Frankenstein* all afternoon. As he scanned his favorite websites, a headline caught his eye: "Hollywood Studio Holds Horror Contest." Max clicked on the article. He saw that the contest was looking for horror movie submissions from young, first-time moviemakers. The winner would get a tour of the movie studio!

Max was getting excited. He already had an idea. He could create a new version of *Frankenstein*! It would combine the book, the movie, and some of Max's own ideas. He asked his friends if they were interested. They were all in!

1. Which is a difference between the book and movie?
   - (A) The monster can speak normally in the book.
   - (B) The monster is frightening looking in the book.
   - (C) The monster does a lot of bad things in the movie.
   - (D) The monster is named Frankenstein in the movie.

2. What is the suffix in the word *normally*?
   - (A) *–ly*
   - (B) *–lly*
   - (C) *norm–*
   - (D) *no–*

3. Which word is a compound word?
   - (A) submission
   - (B) headline
   - (C) contest
   - (D) combine

4. What does Max decide to do?
   - (A) perform a play
   - (B) write a book
   - (C) enter a contest
   - (D) research horror movies

Name: ______________________________ Date: ____________

Directions: Read the text, and answer the questions.

Circle words that describe the characters' actions.

Taking Directions

Max was excited to get started. He listed different jobs on a paper and told his friends, "Write your name next to the job you want."

The list included a variety of jobs: writer, photographer, and set designer were just a few. But right away, there were problems.

Ella asked Max, "How come director isn't listed? I'd like to direct."

"I'm the director because this was all my idea," Max said.

Ella frowned and said, "Okay, fine. I'll write the script."

Lucas asked, "What's a producer?"

Max said, "Producers solve problems during the filming. We don't have a fancy camera, just phone cameras, so you might have to troubleshoot issues we run into."

Lucas groaned. "That sounds boring. Can I be in charge of food?"

Their other friends agreed to act. Finally, the list was filled out. Max was pumped!

Max said to his crew, "Our movie will definitely win the contest!"

1. What genre would this text be considered?
   - (A) fantasy
   - (B) historical fiction
   - (C) science fiction
   - (D) realistic fiction

2. Which job would be in charge of the way actors dressed?
   - (A) producer
   - (B) photographer
   - (C) makeup artist
   - (D) costume designer

3. Why does Max want to be the director?

____

4. How would you describe Max? Use the text to support your answer.

____

____

Name: ________________________________ Date: ________________

Circle words that describe the characters' actions.

Lights! Camera! Action!

Max was ready to shoot the movie in the high school auditorium. He stood on the stage with Ella's finished script and called her over.

"Ella, you didn't make the changes I wanted to the script," Max said.

"Well, that's because it sounds better my way," Ella said.

Max narrowed his eyes and replied, "This movie is my idea, so you need to rewrite this part."

Just then, Lucas came over and said, "The script is looking great, Ella!"

Then, other people came over and started congratulating Ella on her script. Max sighed and walked toward the back of the stage.

Brett was making set decorations, and he called Max over to him. He asked Max, "How should I build a laboratory in a castle?"

Max shrugged nervously, realizing he had no idea.

The next day, Brett brought in a castle interior made of painted cardboard.

"Awesome!" exclaimed Max. "It's way better than I imagined."

Then, Max told Frankie, the costume designer, that the actors should be dressed in everyday clothes. But she disagreed with him. Max almost got into an argument with her, but then he remembered the work Brett had done. He swallowed his pride. A few days later, when Max saw the spooky costumes Frankie had created, he gushed over them. They were perfect!

Cory, who was in charge of lighting, said, "There isn't enough light on set."

Max replied, "I like it dark. It's a horror film."

Cory showed him a sample shot on his phone. You could hardly see the faces of the actors!

"You're right," said Max. "I guess I was wrong."

As the film crew worked through the script, Max realized he had been wrong about a lot of things. He had to admit that making a movie involved serious teamwork.

Max sent his finished movie to the contest, and weeks later, he learned it had won! He told his team that they were going to Hollywood!

Name: ______________________________ Date: ______________

Directions: Read "Lights! Camera! Action!" Then, answer the questions.

1. What does the phrase *swallowed his pride* mean?
   - (A) to eat something that tastes bad
   - (B) to do something even if it will be embarrassing
   - (C) to step down from being in charge
   - (D) to be kind to someone who isn't a friend

2. Which suffix does **not** belong on the word *finish*?
   - (A) *–es*
   - (B) *–ed*
   - (C) *–ing*
   - (D) *–est*

3. How could Brett, the set designer, be described?
   - (A) bossy
   - (B) friendly
   - (C) lazy
   - (D) creative

4. What lesson does Max learn while making the movie?
   - (A) Good workers must be paid for their time.
   - (B) Making movies is expensive.
   - (C) Movies need many talented people to be successful.
   - (D) The director's job is most important.

5. Describe how each of Max's friends help with the movie.

Ella	
Brett	
Frankie	
Cory	

Unit 8
WEEK 2
DAY
5

Name: ______________________ Date: ______________

Directions: Reread "Lights! Camera! Action!" Then, respond to the prompt.

Max is full of ambition. Write a paragraph describing his character traits in detail. Share at least two character traits. Use examples from the text to support each one. For the conclusion, explain why you would or would not want to work on Max's movie.

Name: ______________________________ Date: ________________

Max's Revised Version of *Frankenstein*

INT. — CASTLE LABORATORY — NIGHT

The electronic equipment in the castle laboratory makes strange noises and lights up. VICTOR FRANKENSTEIN is turning some dials on the equipment. The MONSTER is stretched out on a table. He isn't moving. ELIZABETH is Victor's assistant. She places a wire next to the monster's head.

VICTOR FRANKENSTEIN

My experiment is almost ready. Elizabeth, get ready. I will send a current into the monster. I'm doing it now!

[A rod near the monster's head lights up. Elizabeth looks astonished.]

ELIZABETH

You've spent years trying to create life, Victor, but now I fear what this creature will become. I hope you know what you're doing.

[The monster sits up abruptly. His face looms large on screen. He looks perplexed.]

MONSTER

What's going on? I was dead a moment ago and now I'm alive. Grrrr! Who are you puny people?

VICTOR FRANKENSTEIN

He's alive! I've done it.

[The monster gets off the table and growls at Victor. Elizabeth is cowering. The monster goes to look in the mirror.]

MONSTER

Did you have to make me look so unattractive? Grrr!

[The monster looks at Elizabeth.]

MONSTER

Is she your girlfriend?

VICTOR FRANKENSTEIN

Yes. Why?

MONSTER

I want a girlfriend, too. Make me one or I will destroy everything dear to you. Also, I'm starving. Get me something to eat, too!

[Victor walks over to Elizabeth and ushers her out of the room.]

VICTOR FRANKENSTEIN

I'm beginning to fear that making this creature wasn't such a great idea.

Name: ________________________________ Date: ________________

Directions: Read the *Frankenstein* script. Then, answer the questions.

1. How are a script and book alike?

- (A) They both have stage directions.
- (B) They both get performed on stage.
- (C) They both have dialogue.
- (D) They both have chapters.

2. How does Elizabeth feel about creating the monster?

- (A) concerned
- (B) excited
- (C) optimistic
- (D) disappointed

3. What is an antonym of *unattractive*?

- (A) handsome
- (B) ugly
- (C) intelligent
- (D) poor

4. Why is the monster unhappy when he comes to life?

- (A) He says he is ugly.
- (B) He is hungry.
- (C) He wants a girlfriend.
- (D) all of the above

5. What is happening at the end of the script?

____

____

____

Name: ______________________________ Date: ____________________

Directions: Closely read these texts. Study the *Frankenstein* script on page 149. Look for things people are afraid of. Write them in the table.

Close-Reading Texts

Fear of Change	My Favorite Monster
Many people moved from farms to cities. People started to work in factories. Some people didn't like the big changes. They saw that there was a lot of sickness, pollution, and poverty. They thought life was becoming too dangerous and stressful. These people thought that humans had gone too far with technology. They were afraid of what would happen if more machines were created.	"What's the scariest movie you've ever seen?" asked Max. Ella said, "I like the classics. My favorite is *Halloween*—the original of course." Lucas said, "*Jaws* is one I still have nightmares about. That shark was crazy scary!" Alexa frowned. "Ugh, definitely the movie with the clown!" Max said, "The most frightening movie I've ever seen is *Frankenstein*."

Fear of Change	
My Favorite Monster	
***Frankenstein* script**	

Name: ______________________________ Date: ______________

Directions: Closely read these texts. Then, compare and contrast the people from the 1800s to Max.

Close-Reading Texts

Fear and Understanding	Lights! Camera! Action!
For example, when cars were first invented, many people were afraid of them. They didn't want to ride in them. Safety was a big concern. But people have learned a lot about cars since then, and they now understand them better. So, most people have stopped being afraid of them. The same thing is true of electricity. In the early 1800s, many people were afraid of electricity. They didn't know how it worked. That made them fearful.	Max was about to start complaining to Lucas, but other people came over and started congratulating Ella on her script. Max sighed and walked toward the back of the stage. Brett was making set decorations, and he called Max over to him. He asked Max, "How should I build a laboratory in a castle?" Max shrugged nervously, realizing he had no idea. The next day, Brett brought in a castle interior made of painted cardboard. "Awesome!" exclaimed Max. "It's way better than I imagined"

People from 1800s **Max**

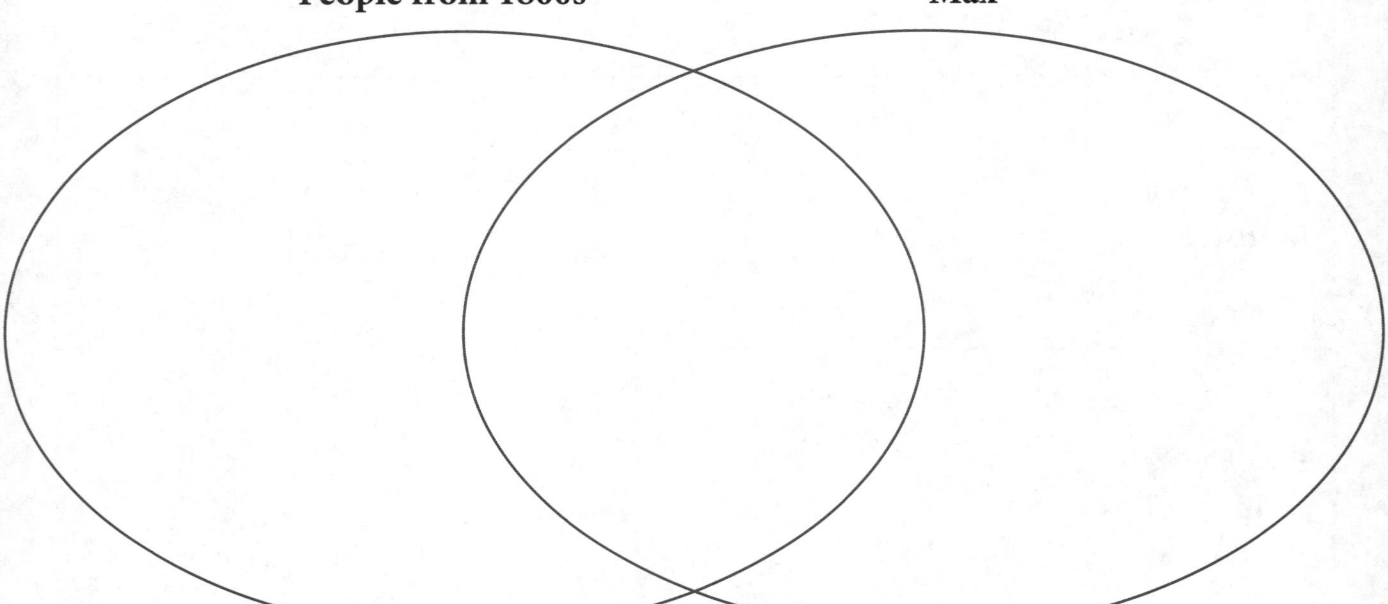

Name: ______________________ Date: ____________

Directions: Think about the text from this unit. Then, respond to the prompt.

Imagine Max's movie wins an award. At the awards show, he has to give an acceptance speech. Think about what Max learned while making his movie and who helped him. Then, write the speech you think he should share with the audience and his friends.

Unit 8
WEEK 3
DAY
5

Name: ______________________ Date: ______________

Directions: Think of a movie or book you enjoy and know well. Write a brief script for a scene in it. The scene can be changed a bit if you wish. It should have two characters with at least six total lines of dialogue. The setting should be described at the beginning and there should be stage directions.

Name: ______________________ Date: ______________

Directions: Read the text, and answer the questions.

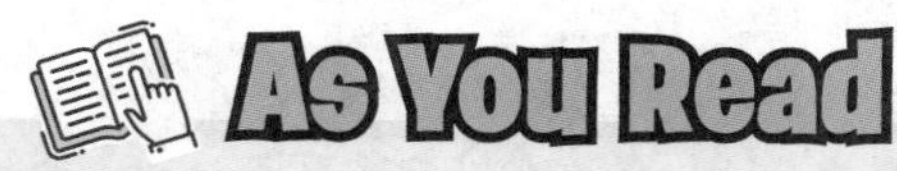

Circle important vocabulary words, and write their meanings to the side.

Your Unique Genes

What color are your eyes, hair, and skin, and how tall are you? All of these things are attributes of your appearance, or the way you look. Now, think about the appearances of your friends and the ways in which they look different from you. Perhaps their eyes are blue, and your eyes are brown. How does that happen, and why do you look the way you look? The answer is because of genes (JEENZ). Genes determine your appearance. Thousands of genes are in each cell of your body. But despite their small size, genes are very important. Genes tell your body what color your eyes, hair, and skin will be. They also determine your height, and they are the reason why everyone looks different. Everyone has their own unique set of genes.

1. Which summarizes the text?
   - (A) Everyone has a different eye color.
   - (B) Genes are not important.
   - (C) Each person has unique genes that control their appearance.
   - (D) Genes are very small; even an ant is larger.

2. Based on the context of the text, *determine* means ______.
   - (A) to dislike
   - (B) to decide
   - (C) to like how something will be
   - (D) to control the limits of

3. Which of the following is a homophone of *genes*?
   - (A) spleens
   - (B) generous
   - (C) genius
   - (D) jeans

4. What is the author's purpose?
   - (A) to entertain
   - (B) to inform
   - (C) to persuade
   - (D) to frighten

Name: ______________________ Date: ______________

Directions: Read the text, and answer the questions.

Circle important vocabulary words, and write their meanings to the side.

The Jobs of Genes

Although genes are extremely small, they have a lot of work to do. Each person has thousands of genes, and each gene has its own special job. For example, think about your eyes: are they brown, blue, green, or some other color? Maybe one of your eyes or one part of your eye is a different color than the other eye. A special gene controls what color your eyes will be. Another gene controls the color of your skin. You may have dark skin or light skin. Everyone has a unique gene that controls what color their skin will be. Genes can even control whether you will have freckles! There is a special gene in charge of your height, too. It tells your body how tall you will be when you grow up. All your genes work together to make you look the way you look.

1. Which word does **not** have a long *e* vowel sound?
   - (A) green
   - (B) gene
   - (C) example
   - (D) maybe

2. Which is **not** determined by a person's genes?
   - (A) eye color
   - (B) T-shirt color
   - (C) skin color
   - (D) hair color

3. Which is another way to say how tall you are?
   - (A) height
   - (B) genes
   - (C) eye color
   - (D) freckles

4. Which title could also be a good fit for the text?
   - (A) Telling My Body
   - (B) Height
   - (C) I Am Tall
   - (D) Your Genes and You

Name: ______________________________ Date: ______________

Directions: Read the text, and answer the questions.

Circle important vocabulary words, and write their meanings to the side.

Passing Down Genes

Where do genes come from, and how do people get them? A person gets their genes from their biological parents. Each parent has physical characteristics. And both parents have thousands of genes. They pass copies of their genes on when they have children. Half of a person's genes come from their mother, and the other half comes from their father. For example, each parent gives their child a gene for eye color. If both parents give a gene for brown eyes, then their child will have brown eyes, too. But imagine that the mother gave a gene for blue eyes and the father gave a gene for brown eyes. The gene for brown eyes is the dominant gene, so the child's eyes will be brown. Still, the child received one eye color gene from each parent.

1. Which is the antonym of *both*?

- (A) some
- (B) neither
- (C) one
- (D) each

2. The term *physical characteristics* means _____.

- (A) how a person looks
- (B) what a person thinks
- (C) the character of a person
- (D) items that have character

3. Where does a person get their genes?

____

____

4. How could someone have a different eye color from a parent?

____

____

____

Name: ______________________ Date: ______________

Circle important vocabulary words. Write their meanings or synonyms to the side.

It's All in the Genes

What do you have in common with a pumpkin, a panda, and a basset hound? The answer is genes! Every living thing has genes, and the set of genes for each living thing is different. That is why you do not look the same as your friends. It is also why you do not look like a pumpkin, a panda, or a basset hound. Your genes are unique to you. They are in charge of your eye color, your hair color, and your height.

Pumpkins have genes, too. Their genes are in charge of their shapes, colors, and leaf sizes. There are genes in every pumpkin seed that tell the seed it will become a pumpkin. These genes ensure that pumpkins will grow instead of other plants if you plant pumpkin seeds.

Just like pumpkins, pandas also have genes. These genes tell a panda's body that it will have black and white fur. They also tell the panda's body that it will have black ears and black circles around its eyes. Mother pandas and father pandas pass those genes on to their babies, just like human parents pass their genes on to their biological children.

A basset hound's genes give it droopy ears, a long body, and short legs. Genes also give basset hounds an excellent sense of smell. Basset hounds are just one breed of dog with its own special genes. Other breeds of dog have different genes. That is why basset hounds do not look like golden retrievers.

Although some living things may look similar to each other, their genes make them different. Each living thing has its own unique set of genes.

Name: ______________________________ Date: ____________________

Directions: Read "It's All in the Genes." Then, answer the questions.

1. Which statement is true?
   - (A) Only some living things have genes.
   - (B) All dogs have the same genes.
   - (C) Each living thing has genes.
   - (D) Children have the same genes as everyone in their family.

2. Which does **not** have genes?
   - (A) water
   - (B) dogs
   - (C) whales
   - (D) ladybugs

3. What is the author's purpose?
   - (A) to tell how genes make living things different
   - (B) to get you to adopt a basset hound
   - (C) to tell how pumpkins grow
   - (D) to tell you where you can go to see pandas

4. A reader can predict that basset hounds will have _____.
   - (A) puppies with very long legs
   - (B) puppies with short ears
   - (C) puppies that do not have a good sense of smell
   - (D) puppies that look like their parents

5. Write what information is given to each living thing from their genes.

Pumpkins	
Panda bears	
Basset hounds	

Name: ______________________________ Date: ______________

Directions: Reread "It's All in the Genes." Then, respond to the prompt.

Write a summary of the passage. Include an important idea from each paragraph of the text. Be sure to include introduction and conclusion sentences in your summary.

Name: ______________________ Date: ______________

Directions: Read the text, and answer the questions.

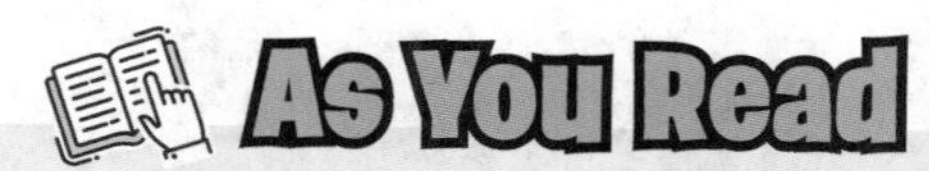

Make a note of one way you personally connect to the text.

The Family Tree

"Please pay attention, class!" Mrs. Allen said.

Rhonda and Stefan kept chatting at the back of the room. As usual, Rhonda was attempting to one-up him. Rhonda stuck out her tongue and then rolled it.

"Can you do that?" she challenged Stefan. He tried as hard as he could, but his tongue wouldn't move like that.

He became curious and wondered whether he could teach himself to roll his tongue. It turned out that this was a trait that was controlled by certain genes, but not everyone had those genes.

The next day in school he performed an experiment.

"Everyone, stick out your tongue and try to curl it," Stefan told the class.

It was a funny sight! Stefan tried not to laugh as he counted how many students rolled their tongues. It was about one-third of the class. He wondered what other genetic traits people exhibited.

1. How should the word *experiment* be broken into syllables?
   - (A) ex·per·i·ment
   - (B) e·xper·i·ment
   - (C) exp·er·i·ment
   - (D) ex·per·im·ent

2. Why does Stefan do the experiment?
   - (A) to win a bet with Rhonda
   - (B) he thinks it is interesting
   - (C) to work on his project
   - (D) because it is his homework

3. What does the word *genes* mean?
   - (A) a physical ability to do something unique
   - (B) a quality that makes one thing better than another
   - (C) part of a cell that controls the way a living thing looks
   - (D) all of a cell

4. How would Stefan best be described?
   - (A) funny
   - (B) kind
   - (C) curious
   - (D) helpful

Name: ______________________ Date: ______________

Directions: Read the text, and answer the questions.

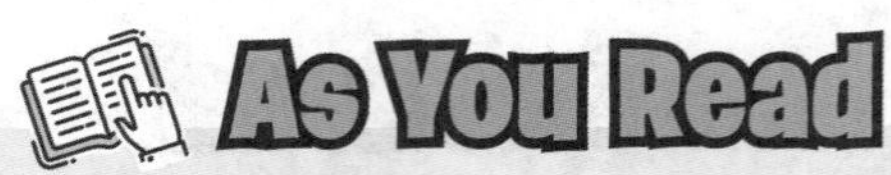

Make a note of one way you personally connect to the text.

Great Traits

After school, Stefan researched different traits that children often inherited from their parents. He made a chart with the names of his classmates in one column and a row of different traits at the top.

At school the next day, Stefan proceeded to check off which traits each person had. He first asked his classmates to hold up their thumbs.

"Whose thumbs are curved?" he asked and checked off their names. "Okay, now whose thumbs are straight?" and listed them.

Next, he asked, "Who has dimples?" He took note of this, too.

Then, he asked who was left-handed and right-handed and recorded the data. When he finished his chart, Stefan made a poster showing each classmate's traits and hung it on the classroom wall.

Stefan got another idea. What if he made a chart for his family's traits?

1. What is a synonym for *data*?
   - (A) information
   - (B) question
   - (C) trait
   - (D) project

2. What does the word *inherit* mean?
   - (A) to receive a trait from the genes of a family member
   - (B) to receive advice from a person
   - (C) a quality that is harmful to a person's health
   - (D) a quality that makes one thing different from another

3. Which word has a suffix?
   - (A) family
   - (B) several
   - (C) asked
   - (D) classmate

4. Which trait does Stefan **not** ask his classmates about?
   - (A) attached or unattached earlobes
   - (B) straight or bent thumb
   - (C) dimples or no dimples
   - (D) right- or left-handed

Name: ______________________ Date: ______________

Directions: Read the text, and answer the questions.

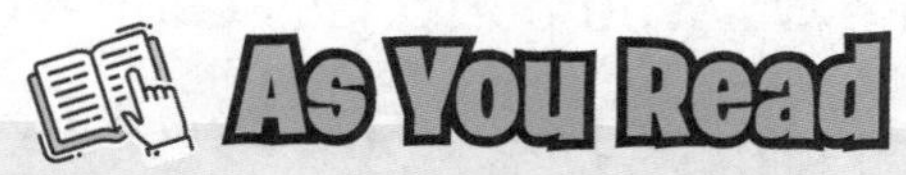

Make a note of one way you personally connect to the text.

Family Matters

Stefan created a chart of traits for members of his family. First, he asked them the same questions that he asked his classmates. He quickly discovered that he did not always share the same traits with his mother, father, and sister. Some traits were pretty obvious. Stefan had brown eyes, just like his father. But his mother and sister had blue eyes. So, he probably got that trait from his father. His mother had freckles, but he and his sister didn't. He had straight dark hair like his dad. His sister and mother had light curly hair.

As Stefan completed his chart, he had another idea. What about the rest of his family: his grandparents, aunts, uncles, and cousins? He called them up to see who had what trait and began to put their answers on a larger chart. Slowly, he began to wonder more about his family history.

1. Which is an antonym of *obvious*?
   - (A) clear
   - (B) data
   - (C) common
   - (D) doubtful

2. Which sentence is true?
   - (A) Stefan has freckles.
   - (B) Stefan and his father have straight hair.
   - (C) Stefan's sister has dark hair.
   - (D) Stefan and his sister have blue eyes.

3. Which of his parents does Stefan's sister seem to look like? Explain your answer.

____

____

4. What do you think Stefan will discover about the traits of the rest of his family?

____

____

Name: ______________________________ Date: ______________

Make a note of one way you personally connect to the text.

A Family Hero

Stefan had a thousand questions. Who passed their traits to his parents? Who were his ancestors? Stefan started by asking about his grandfather.

"My father was born in Italy," said Stefan's father. "He moved to Pennsylvania as a boy. If you want to learn more, we have papers stored away."

In the attic, Stefan found some cardboard boxes. One box had a surprising photo. It showed his Grandpa Rocco in a Navy uniform, and it was dated 1943. He had fought in World War II! Stefan had no idea. Next, Stefan found a small cloth box that contained a fancy medal shaped like a gold cross.

Stefan's father said, "Oh, that's my father's Navy Cross. He died when I was a teenager. I never got to ask him about that."

Stefan discovered that the Navy Cross was given to men who showed incredible bravery during wartime. How did he earn the medal? Grandma had died, so he had to find out another way.

A second photo showed a ship with the date 1942 on the back and the name *Frank*. Stefan could read letters and numbers on the ship's hull. According to a website, they were a code for a ship sunk in 1944. But who was Frank?

Stefan's father said, "You could ask your Great Uncle Joe, your Grandpa Rocco's younger brother."

I feel like a detective in a mystery, thought Stefan, *and I want to solve it.*

On the phone, his great uncle said, "I remember a Frank…Frank Bergen. He used to talk to your Grandpa Rocco about the war. I wasn't too interested."

Great Uncle Joe gave Frank's phone number to Stefan, and Stefan called him. Frank agreed to meet Stefan with his father.

"Rocco and I were shipmates on a battleship," said Frank. "One day in 1944, an enemy plane dropped a bomb on the ship. Though he was wounded, Rocco saved a bunch of sailors from a fire. After the ship sank, he was on a lifeboat by himself, pulling men out of the water all day and night. He saved a lot of lives, including mine!"

"There might be other secrets in our family tree," Stefan told his father. "I can't wait to find out!"

Name: ______________________________ Date: ________________

Directions: Read "A Family Hero." Then, answer the questions.

1. What could Stefan inherit from his grandfather?

- (A) being in the Navy
- (B) earning a Navy Cross
- (C) hair length
- (D) eye color

2. Who tells Stefan how his grandfather earned a Navy Cross?

- (A) Rocco
- (B) Frank
- (C) Uncle Joe
- (D) his father

3. What does the word *ancestor* mean in the text?

- (A) a brave person
- (B) a soldier
- (C) a family member from the past
- (D) an expert at research

4. Which is a synonym of *fancy*?

- (A) decorative
- (B) dull
- (C) small
- (D) boring

5. Write the steps Stefan takes to get in touch with the person who could tell him about his grandfather.

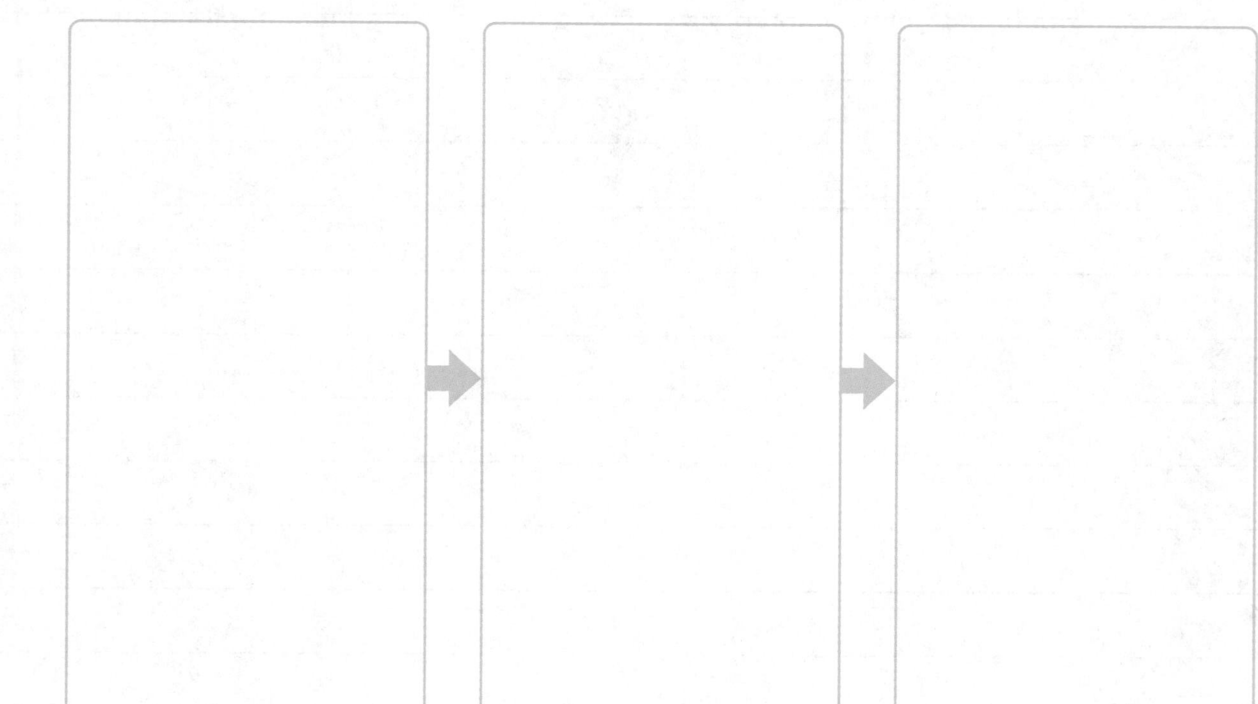

Name: ______________________ Date: ______________

Directions: Reread "A Family Hero." Then, respond to the prompt.

Imagine your grandchildren someday ask about your childhood. Think of something interesting, funny, scary, or educational that has happened to you. Write a story about it. Describe the event so you can someday pass on the memory to a younger family member.

Name: ______________________ Date: ______________

See Your Own DNA

Our genes tell our bodies what they will look like and how they will work. But what are genes made of? The answer is a chemical called DNA. This stands for deoxyribonucleic (dee-AHK-sih-ry-boh-new-klee-ihk) acid. DNA is in almost every cell of the body. It contains a code. This code allows genes to pass down traits. DNA is very small. But this experiment lets you see a strand of this amazing chemical.

What You Need

- water
- measuring cup and spoons
- clear dish soap
- food coloring (any color)
- salt
- rubbing alcohol (at least 70%)
- clear cups
- toothpicks

What You Do

1. In a cup, mix 17 ounces (500 milliliters) of water with one tablespoon of salt. Stir it until the salt dissolves.
2. In a different cup, pour 3 tablespoons of this mixture. Gargle it in your mouth for about one minute. Spit the water back into the cup.
3. Stir a drop of soap into the liquid you gargled.
4. In another clean cup, add the alcohol and three drops of food coloring.
5. Tilt the cup you gargled in and add to it the alcohol. Try not to mix the two layers.
6. Let the mixture sit for about two and a half minutes.

What You See

White strings or clumps should appear in the cup. That is your DNA! They came from cells in your cheeks that came off when you gargled. Use a toothpick to pick up the DNA for a close-up look at the building blocks of your body!

Name: ______________________________ Date: ________________

Directions: Read "See Your Own DNA." Then, answer the questions.

1. Which is **not** a necessary supply for the experiment?

- (A) water
- (B) salt
- (C) rubbing alcohol
- (D) baking soda

2. How many syllables are in the word *different*?

- (A) two
- (B) four
- (C) one
- (D) three

3. According to the directions, what should you do after you gargle and spit?

- (A) Measure one tablespoon of salt.
- (B) Add a few drops of food coloring.
- (C) Stir a drop of soap into the liquid.
- (D) Mix it with rubbing alcohol.

4. What is the end goal of the experiment?

- (A) To see a clump of your DNA.
- (B) To look at your DNA under a microscope.
- (C) To dye your DNA with food coloring.
- (D) To know how your DNA shapes how you look.

5. What is DNA? Use the text to help explain your response.

____

____

____

Name: ______________________________ Date: ______________

Directions: Closely read these texts. Reread the experiment on page 167. Look for two important words from each text. Complete the table using the words you find.

Close-Reading Texts

Passing Down Genes	The Family Tree
Where do genes come from, and how do people get them? A person gets their genes from their biological parents. Each parent has physical characteristics. And both parents have thousands of genes. They pass copies of their genes on when they have children. Half of a person's genes come from their mother, and the other half comes from their father.	The next day in school he performed an experiment. "Everyone, stick out your tongue and try to curl it," Stefan told the class. It was a funny sight! Stefan tried not to laugh as he counted how many students rolled their tongues. It was about one-third of the class. He wondered what other genetic traits people exhibited.

Text	Word 1 and Definition	Word 2 and Definition
Passing Down Genes		
The Family Tree		
See Your Own DNA		

Name: ______________________ Date: ______________

Directions: Closely read these texts. Answer the questions to compare the texts.

Close-Reading Texts

Passing Down Genes	Family Matters
Half of a person's genes come from their mother, and the other half comes from their father. For example, each parent gives their child a gene for eye color. If both parents give a gene for brown eyes, then their child will have brown eyes, too. But imagine that the mother gave a gene for blue eyes and the father gave a gene for brown eyes. The gene for brown eyes is the dominant gene, so the child's eyes will be brown.	He quickly discovered that he did not always share the same traits with his mother, father, and sister. Some traits were pretty obvious. Stefan had brown eyes, just like his father. But his mother and sister had blue eyes. So, he probably got that trait from his father. His mother had freckles, but he and his sister didn't. He had straight dark hair like his dad. His sister and mother had light curly hair.

What do the paragraphs have in common?

____

____

____

____

What different information do the paragraphs have?

____

____

____

____

____

____

Name: ______________________________ Date: ______________

Directions: Think about the text from this unit. Then, respond to the prompt.

Family members sometimes resemble each other. This is not just in the way they look. They might have the same interests and hobbies, sense of style, or personality traits. Think about the people in your family. Write a paragraph describing ways you are similar to and different from them. Your paragraph should have at least three examples of compare or contrast.

Name: ______________________ Date: ____________

Directions: Think of something you can explain how to do. It might be doing a science experiment, cooking or baking, playing a sport, or doing a hobby. Complete the information below to write directions for someone else, and draw a picture.

Directions to ______________________

What You Need

____

____

____

____

____

____

What You Do

____

____

____

____

____

____

____

____

What You End With

____

____

____

____

____

Name: ______________________ Date: ______________

Directions: Read the text, and answer the questions.

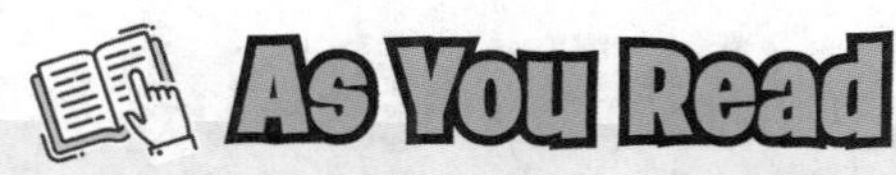

Draw a simple picture in the margin to show the main idea.

Moving Air

Air is constantly moving. Sometimes, air moves north from the Gulf of Mexico. That air is warm and moist because the Gulf of Mexico is warm and moist. Sometimes, air moves south from Canada. That air is cool and dry because it comes from a cool, dry place. Sometimes, a mass of warm, moist air meets a mass of cool, dry air. When that happens, the air masses become unstable and can change quickly. Strong winds can begin to blow. If winds blow fast enough and change direction, they can become storms and begin to spin, just as water does when it goes down a drain. If a spinning storm doesn't touch the ground, it is called a *funnel*. But if the funnel does touch the ground, it is called a *tornado*. Tornadoes are common in areas where masses of warm and cool air meet.

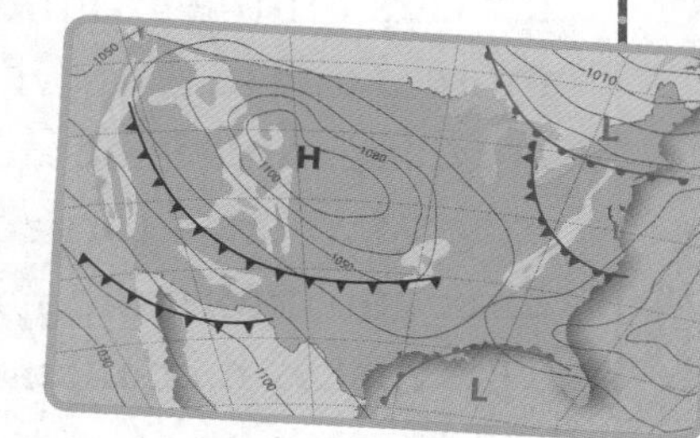

1. Which question might a reader ask after reading this text?

- (A) Where does cool air come from?
- (B) Does the Gulf of Mexico try to keep its warm air?
- (C) Why can't warm and cool air mix and still be stable?
- (D) all of the above

2. Which is an antonym of *moist*?

- (A) cold
- (B) dry
- (C) hot
- (D) spinning

3. Which of the following would best accompany this text?

- (A) a video showing a tornado forming
- (B) a video of wind in Canada
- (C) a video of cool air being measured by scientists
- (D) a video of the Gulf of Mexico in the summer

4. What is the tone of the text?

- (A) formal
- (B) informal
- (C) scary
- (D) silly

Name: ______________________ Date: ______________

Directions: Read the text, and answer the questions.

Draw a simple picture in the margin to show the main idea.

Dangerous Winds

Why are tornadoes dangerous? There are two big reasons. One reason is the wind that comes with tornadoes. The strong winds that form tornadoes move upward. As they spin, they carry things along with them. Some tornadoes are weak. Their winds carry leaves, branches, and dust with them. Other tornadoes are stronger. The winds from strong tornadoes can break windows. They can pull up trees. Very strong tornadoes can knock over buildings and lift cars off the ground. The bigger and stronger tornadoes are, the more damage they will cause. The second reason why tornadoes are dangerous is because they are unpredictable. It is hard to tell exactly where a tornado will strike. It is also hard to tell which direction a tornado will go. They move and form very quickly. This makes it challenging to warn people before a tornado comes.

1. Which question is most related to the text?

Ⓐ Do large earthquakes cause more damage than tornadoes?

Ⓑ How fast do tornadoes move?

Ⓒ Can scientists tell which direction a hurricane is moving?

Ⓓ Do hurricanes pull up trees?

2. Another word for *damage* is _____.

Ⓐ building Ⓒ harm

Ⓑ reward Ⓓ anger

3. What is the root word in *unpredictable*?

Ⓐ predict

Ⓑ table

Ⓒ unpredict

Ⓓ redictable

4. What is something a tornado cannot do?

Ⓐ cause an earthquake

Ⓑ break windows

Ⓒ lift cars

Ⓓ knock over buildings

Name: ______________________ Date: ______________

Directions: Read the text, and answer the questions.

Draw a simple picture in the margin to show the main idea.

Tornado Safety Tips

If you hear a tornado warning, it means that a tornado has touched ground. You need to take shelter right away. Here is what to do if you hear a tornado warning:

- Go to a basement if one is available to you. You can also go inside a room far away from windows, such as a bathroom or a closet.
- If you can, get under a sturdy piece of furniture, such as a table.

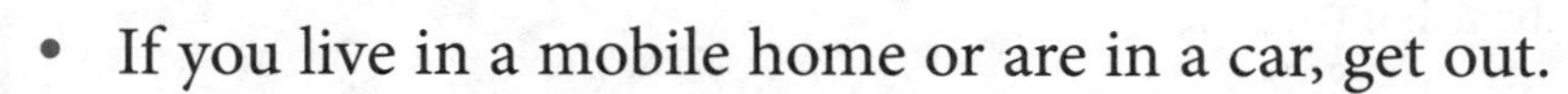

- If you live in a mobile home or are in a car, get out.
- If you're outside, go to a ditch or a low-lying area and lie flat in it.
- Stay away from fallen power lines and damaged areas.

1. Which is **not** a good place to take shelter from a tornado?

Ⓐ in a car

Ⓑ in a basement

Ⓒ under a sturdy table

Ⓓ in a closet

2. Which word is an antonym of *dangerous*?

Ⓐ risky

Ⓑ deadly

Ⓒ secure

Ⓓ none of the above

3. What does it mean to *take shelter*?

____

____

4. Where would you go in your home if you heard a tornado warning? Explain your reasoning.

____

____

Name: ______________________ Date: ______________

Draw simple pictures in the margin to show the main idea for each paragraph.

Storm Chasers

Some people track, or follow, big storms. These people are often called storm chasers. Their goal is to get as close as they can to storms so that they can observe and record them. They find out where storms are happening. Then, they travel to those places to watch the storms, take pictures, and record videos of them.

Some storm chasers follow tornadoes. They use equipment to learn about the tornado they are chasing. Their equipment can show how fast a tornado is moving and the direction it is headed. Their equipment also measures how fast the wind is blowing inside a tornado.

What kind of people become storm chasers? Some storm chasers are scientists. They want to study tornadoes. Other storm chasers track storms because it is their hobby. They find storms very interesting and want to know more about them. Some of them get a thrill seeing the storms up close and in action. A few storm chasers are paid to chase storms. They sell their videos and pictures. They may even offer storm-chasing tours! But most storm chasers are not paid. They chase storms simply because they are passionate about them.

Storm chasers travel long distances looking for storms. They spend a lot of time in their vehicles. They have to be good at using cameras, computers, and other equipment. They also have to be good at recording data. Storm chasers start by checking their computers. They find out where a tornado might hit based on weather conditions. Then, they travel to that place. On the way, they check their computers again. Finally, they get to a place where a tornado might strike. When they do, they stop and set up their equipment. They also look at the sky to see if a tornado will form. If a tornado does form, they observe, take pictures, and then get out of the way. If no tornado forms, they move on to another place.

It is not easy to be a storm chaser. It is dangerous and unpredictable. But it can also be exciting!

Name: ______________________ Date: ______________

Directions: Read "Storm Chasers." Then, answer the questions.

1. After having read this text, a reader might _____.
   - (A) decide to stay inside forever so as to avoid storms
   - (B) become more interested in the science of volcanoes
   - (C) decide to study the science of animals and living things
   - (D) none of the above

2. Which do storm chasers probably like?
   - (A) science
   - (B) history
   - (C) tennis
   - (D) music

3. What is storm chasing like?
   - (A) Storm chasing is quick and easy for most storm chasers. It is also exciting.
   - (B) Storm chasing can be done at home. That is why it is exciting.
   - (C) Storm chasing is mostly done by people who are paid to chase storms.
   - (D) Storm chasing takes a lot of travel and is not easy, but it can be exciting.

4. Based on the text, which items does a storm chaser need?
   - (A) rain jacket, computer with GPS tracking, a truck with rain tires
   - (B) rain jacket, a rubber duck, a computer with GPS tracking
   - (C) a rubber duck, a truck with rain tires, a car with rain tires
   - (D) a truck with rain tires, a cotton sweater, a public telephone

5. Write the steps a storm chaser takes when chasing a storm.

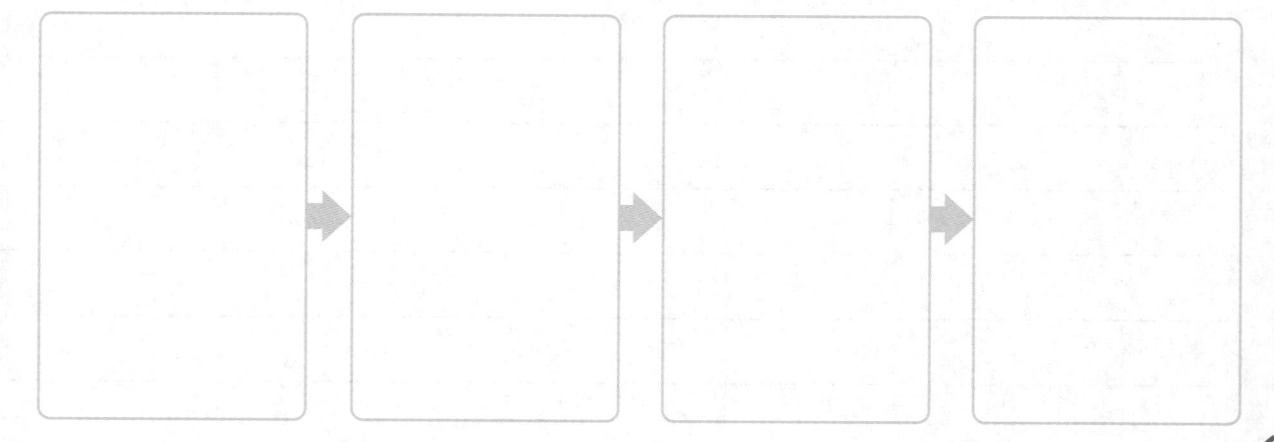

Name: ______________________________ **Date:** ______________

Directions: Reread "Storm Chasers." Then, respond to the prompt.

Pretend you are a storm chaser who had a very exciting and successful chase last night! Write a journal entry to describe how you found the storm and what happened while you were there.

Name: ______________________ Date: ______________

Directions: Read the text, and answer the questions.

Circle words or phrases that help describe the setting.

A New Route

It was a beautiful autumn afternoon. Tricia decided to go home from school by taking a new route. Usually, she walked home using the most direct route, which was three blocks south and eight blocks west. But today, it was just too beautiful to go directly home. This time, she went two blocks north, and then eight blocks west. Tricia was about to turn south toward her house when she saw a creek with a small stream of water running through it on the left side of the road.

Tricia crossed the street and went to the bank of the creek. She looked up and down the bank, but she didn't see anyone nearby. Tricia thought to herself, *I had no idea there was a creek here. It's hard to believe it's right here in the middle of the city. What a wonderful place!*

1. Which is a synonym for *route*?
   - Ⓐ way
   - Ⓑ creek
   - Ⓒ river
   - Ⓓ block

2. Which word has the same vowel sound as *through*?
   - Ⓐ blocks
   - Ⓑ too
   - Ⓒ looked
   - Ⓓ thought

3. Tricia learns that on the different route home, ______.
   - Ⓐ there are more trees
   - Ⓑ there is a pond
   - Ⓒ there is a creek
   - Ⓓ there are fewer trees

4. What does the *most direct route* mean?
   - Ⓐ the longest way
   - Ⓑ the straightest way
   - Ⓒ the prettiest way
   - Ⓓ the cheapest way

Name: ______________________________ Date: ________________

Directions: Read the text, and answer the questions.

Circle words or phrases that help describe the setting.

At the Creek

Tricia sat on the bank of the creek and took it all in. The green moss Tricia used as a seat was as soft as velvet and very comfortable. The clouds in the sky were puffy and floated lazily by. Tricia could see the tall trees on the creek banks as they swayed gently in the breeze. They were slowly losing their orange, red, and yellow leaves. Tricia liked watching the sparkling creek water and hearing it rush softly by. She saw a few frogs hopping around, and she even saw a salamander slither by! She saw turtles, too, and a lot of insects buzzing across the surface of the water.

The creek was alive with the noises of the creatures who lived there. It felt so peaceful. Tricia wished she could live at the creek, too.

1. The setting of the text is a creek, but it could also take place at ______.
   - Ⓐ a pond
   - Ⓑ a beach
   - Ⓒ a school
   - Ⓓ a factory

2. Which is a synonym for *swayed*?
   - Ⓐ stayed
   - Ⓑ stood
   - Ⓒ swung
   - Ⓓ grew

3. Which shows the correct pronunciation of *salamander*?
   - Ⓐ sal-UH-man-der
   - Ⓑ SAL-uh-man-der
   - Ⓒ sal-uh-MAN-der
   - Ⓓ sal-uh-man-DER

4. Which of these is a simile?
   - Ⓐ alive with noise
   - Ⓑ as soft as velvet
   - Ⓒ croaking frogs
   - Ⓓ at the creek

Name: ______________________ Date: ______________

Directions: Read the text, and answer the questions.

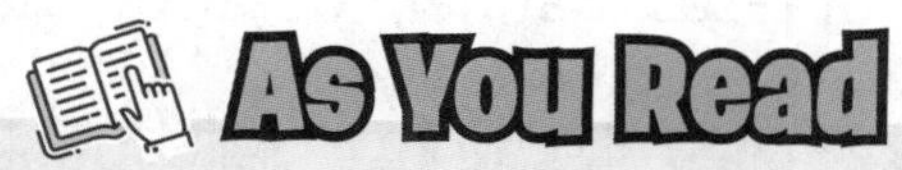

Circle words or phrases that help describe the setting.

Inviting a Friend

Tricia invited her best friend Lisa to see the creek she had discovered. So one Saturday morning, the two girls headed there together. Tricia wasn't sure Lisa would like the creek because she always complained about being out in nature, but when they got there, Lisa said, "Wow, this is so beautiful!"

At the creek, Tricia could observe the water and the animals and listen to the sounds they made. She often brought a book to read and would sit with it on the bank, listening to the flowing water. The creek had become her favorite place. Lisa thought it was wonderful, too.

"We should have a picnic here," Lisa said eagerly. "We could bring our lunch and spend the whole afternoon here. What do you think?"

"That's an awesome idea!" Tricia answered. "Let's come here next weekend."

1. The first sentence suggests the text is about _____.
   - (A) two friends visiting a pond and the fun things they do
   - (B) two friends visiting a creek and the activities they do
   - (C) two friends visiting a house and having a picnic there
   - (D) two friends visiting a creek and playing on the swing

2. Which words have the same suffix?
   - (A) lucky and Saturday
   - (B) peaceful and wonderful
   - (C) certainly and beautiful
   - (D) none of the above

3. How does Lisa feel about the creek?

   ____
   ____
   ____

4. Why do you think Tricia invited Lisa to the creek?

   ____
   ____

Name: ______________________ Date: ______________

Circle words or phrases that help describe the setting.

A Very Wet Picnic

That very next Saturday, Tricia and Lisa went back to their new favorite place—the creek. Each girl had a backpack that was crammed full of food and supplies. Tricia also brought a camera, a blanket, and a large bottle of water with her. Lisa brought two cans of soda, a pad of paper, and some pens.

When the girls arrived at the creek, Tricia pulled the blanket out of her backpack. Lisa helped her set it on the ground, and they started to unpack their food. They shared their food, talking and laughing about the events of the school week.

When they finished eating, Tricia said, "Let's take some pictures."

Lisa agreed, and they walked up and down the creek. They took pictures of frogs and turtles. They took pictures of some salamanders, colorful leaves, and countless flowers that surrounded them.

Then, Tricia and Lisa decided to draw their surroundings. They drew trees and rocks, the water in the creek, and some of the animals, too. All of a sudden, Lisa saw a drop fall on her paper. Then, she saw another drop.

"It's starting to rain, Tricia," Lisa said in a panicked voice. "We need to leave, or we'll get soaked!"

The two girls quickly stuffed everything back in their backpacks. The rain was starting to come down harder, and the wind was starting to blow. They shrugged their backpacks on and sprinted as fast as they could back to their neighborhood. By that time, the storm had worsened. Rain lashed at the windows and thunder boomed. When they got to Tricia's house, they raced inside, dripping water across the floor as they went.

"What happened to you two?" asked Tricia's mother.

"We got caught in the rainstorm," Tricia gasped.

Tricia's mother got the two girls some dry towels. Lisa and Tricia looked at each other and laughed.

"At least we took pictures of our picnic before the rain!" Lisa said thankfully.

Name: ________________________________ Date: ________________

Directions: Read "A Very Wet Picnic." Then, answer the questions.

1. What happens as the girls are drawing?
   - (A) It starts to rain.
   - (B) Lisa's drink spills.
   - (C) A salamander approaches them.
   - (D) They decide to take pictures.

2. The purpose of reading this text is _____.
   - (A) to read about rain and wet grass
   - (B) to read about what a picnic is
   - (C) to read a story about how to draw animals
   - (D) to read a story about two friends

3. Why do you think Tricia and Lisa run as fast as they can?
   - (A) They are late for dinner.
   - (B) They are afraid of the dark.
   - (C) They saw something scary at the creek.
   - (D) They want to stay dry.

4. This story is an example of _____.
   - (A) characters goofing around without planning anything out
   - (B) characters making plans and keeping them without any changes
   - (C) characters making plans but having to change them
   - (D) none of the above

5. Describe the problem and solution of the story.

Problem	**Solution**

Unit 10
WEEK 2
DAY
5

Name: ______________________________ Date: ______________

Directions: Reread "A Very Wet Picnic." Then, respond to the prompt.

The story ends with Tricia and Lisa back at Tricia's house. But what happens next? Continue the story of the girls' rainy afternoon together. Before you begin writing, ask yourself questions such as: What do the girls do? Does it stop raining? Were their things ruined?

Name: ______________________________ Date: ____________

Weather Report Transmission

[Voice of Stan Hail, weatherman]

"Folks, this is Stan Hail with the Weather Report. We're about to go to a live report from storm chaser Sandra Cane. She and her crew are driving in a special van to get as close as possible to some wild tornadoes. You're on the air, Sandra."

[Voice of Sandra Cane]

"Stan, I'm reporting from Highway 16, just outside the town of Ithaka. The crew with me in the storm chaser truck is videotaping a huge black spinning cloud called a super cell not too far from here. A funnel is beginning to form at the bottom of the cloud. It's snaking down...and it hit the ground. We've officially got a tornado!"

[Voice of Stan Hail, weatherman]

"Wow, what more can you tell us, Sandra?"

[Voice of Sandra Cane]

"It's looking about as wide as a school building, and our radar clocks its spin at a speed of 185 miles (298 kilometers) an hour. That makes it an EF-4 rating. The tornado seems to be moving east, so that's where we're heading. And it's starting to hail, Stan, we've got large chunks of ice the size of ping-pong balls falling around us. The wind is picking up and the skies are very dark, with lots of lightning strikes. Sorry, Stan. Give me a minute."

[Voice of Stan Hail, weatherman]

"No problem. Let us know what else you're seeing."

[Voice of Sandra Cane]

"Definitely. We're getting close to the twister now. Wow! It just tore up a group of trees, sending them up the funnel. It's raining pretty hard now, and we're just up the road from the twister. It's sounding like a roaring train right now. It seems to be moving along the highway in our direction, so we're going to meet head on in no time. It's amazing, the tornado seems to be getting wider, it's like a moving wall of black air. Wow, it just picked up a car! Did you get a shot of that, guys? It's almost on us! Our truck is shaking like crazy. Debris is flying everywhere. We'd better park [sound indistinct] this underpass while the twister moves over us. It's louder than a jet plane taking off [sound indistinct]. I hope...

[Voice of Stan Hail]

"Well, we lost Sandra. I hope she and her friends are safe. Sandra, if you're hearing this, give us a call and let us know you are safe. Now, it's time for our Sports Report."

Name: ______________________________ Date: ________________

Directions: Read "Weather Report Transmission." Then, answer the questions.

1. Why is Sandra Cane chasing a storm?
   - (A) for a magazine article
   - (B) to research earthquakes
   - (C) for a radio news report
   - (D) to rescue a stranded person

2. What is the root word of *snaking*?
   - (A) snack
   - (B) snake
   - (C) snak
   - (D) shack

3. What does *debris* mean?
   - (A) leftover pieces after something has been destroyed
   - (B) heavy precipitation, such as hail
   - (C) types of transportation
   - (D) an instrument used to measure tornadoes

4. How is the tornado described in the story?
   - (A) a moving brick wall
   - (B) a moving wall of black air
   - (C) ping-pong ball-sized chunks of ice
   - (D) a small, slow funnel

5. Write details Sandra shared about the tornado.

Name: ______________________________ Date: ________________

Directions: Closely read these texts. Study the radio transmission on page 185. Write words and phrases that describe the storms from each text.

Close-Reading Texts

Dangerous Winds	A Very Wet Picnic
Some tornadoes are weak. Their winds carry leaves, branches, and dust with them. Other tornadoes are stronger. The winds from strong tornadoes can break windows. They can pull up trees. Very strong tornadoes can knock over buildings and lift cars off the ground. The bigger and stronger tornadoes are, the more damage they will cause. The second reason why tornadoes are dangerous is because they are unpredictable.	The rain was starting to come down harder, and the wind was starting to blow. They shrugged their backpacks on and sprinted as fast as they could back to their neighborhood. By that time, the storm had worsened. Rain lashed at the windows and thunder boomed. When they got to Tricia's house, they raced inside, dripping water across the floor as they went.

Title	Storm Description
Dangerous Winds	
A Very Wet Picnic	
Radio Transmission	

Name: ______________________________ Date: ______________

Directions: Read these texts. Compare and contrast the information shared in each.

Close-Reading Texts

Storm Chasers	Radio Transmission
Storm chasers start by checking their computers. They find out where a tornado might hit based on weather conditions. Then, they travel to that place. On the way, they check their computers again. Finally, they get to a place where a tornado might strike. When they do, they stop and set up their equipment. They also look at the sky to see if a tornado will form. If a tornado does form, they observe, take pictures, and then get out of the way. If no tornado forms, they move on to another place.	"The crew with me in the storm chaser truck is videotaping a huge black spinning cloud called a super cell not too far from here. A funnel is beginning to form at the bottom of the cloud. It's snaking down...and it hit the ground. We've officially got a tornado!" "It's looking about as wide as a school building, and our radar clocks its spin at a speed of 185 miles (298 kilometers) an hour. That makes it an EF-4 rating. The tornado seems to be moving east, so that's where we're heading."

Storm Chasers	Radio Transmission

Both

Name: ______________________ **Date:** ____________

Directions: Think about the texts from this unit. Then, respond to the prompt.

Would you want to be a storm chaser? Write a paragraph explaining why you would or would not want this job. Your paragraph should clearly state your opinion and give three details to support it. It should have a conclusion sentence as well.

Name: ______________________________ Date: ______________

Directions: Think of another segment for the news radio show. The news might be a local event, sports, or a special announcement. Write the broadcast of what the reporters say.

Name: ______________________________ Date: ________________

Directions: Read the text, and answer the questions.

Write one clarifying question you have about the text in the margin.

Different Times

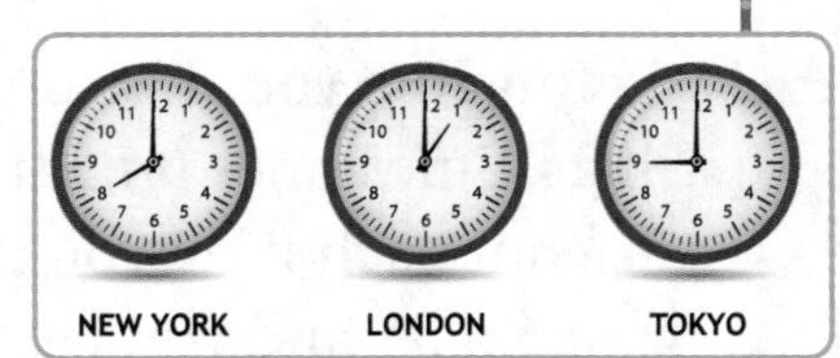

"What time is it?" The answer depends on where you live. There are 24 time zones in the world. Because Earth rotates on its axis, the sun strikes different parts of it at different times. So it wouldn't make sense for the whole world to follow the same time zone.

The United States has several time zones. Each one is an hour apart. As you go east, it gets later. As you go west, it gets earlier. So, it is earlier in California than it is in New York. Some time zone borders follow the borders of the states, but some time zone borders do not. This means there are some states that have two time zones!

When it's the middle of the afternoon in Europe, people in California are just waking up. When it's breakfast time in New York, it's almost lunchtime in London. So, next time you're sitting down to eat lunch, think about other time zones. Somewhere else in the world, kids are getting ready to go to bed.

1. Which sentence is true?

- (A) As you go east, it gets later; as you go west, it gets earlier.
- (B) When it is breakfast in London, it is lunchtime in New York.
- (C) There are 22 time zones in the world.
- (D) The United States has only one time zone.

2. Which word is not plural?

- (A) axis
- (B) kids
- (C) places
- (D) zones

3. Another word for *rotates* is _____.

- (A) grows
- (B) opens
- (C) follows
- (D) turns

4. The phrase *the sun strikes* means that

- (A) the sun runs out of fuel
- (B) the sun shines on
- (C) the sun is violent
- (D) the sun is round

Name: ______________________________ Date: ________________

Directions: Read the text, and answer the questions.

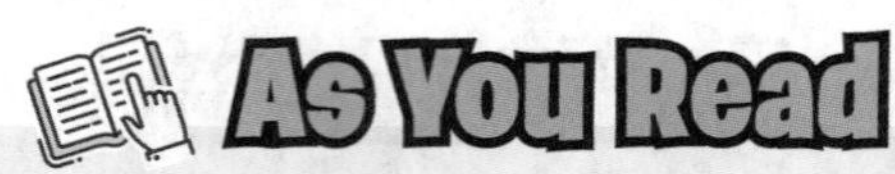

Write one clarifying question you have about the text in the margin.

International Date Line

Imagine you fly around the world starting from New York. You fly through all 24 time zones on Earth. You fly west, so it gets earlier as you go, and you gain an hour each time you pass through a time zone. Now, imagine you finished your flight, and you land back in New York. Does that mean you land on the same day you left? No—you have been in the plane for 24 hours, so it is a day later. How can that be if you gained an hour for each time zone? The answer is the International Date Line. The International Date Line is an imaginary line like the equator. It runs from north to south through the Pacific Ocean, and this line divides one day from the next day. So if it is Wednesday on the east side of the line, it is Thursday on the west side.

1. What happens as you fly west?

- (A) You get motion sickness.
- (B) You fly too fast.
- (C) You gain an hour at each time zone.
- (D) You go to the wrong place.

2. *Earlier* and *later* are ______.

- (A) antonyms
- (B) synonyms
- (C) rhymes
- (D) nouns

3. Which syllable is stressed in the word *imaginary*?

- (A) the first syllable
- (B) the second syllable
- (C) the third syllable
- (D) the fourth syllable

4. The author most likely wrote this to ______.

- (A) entertain an audience and talk about time
- (B) inform an audience about the International Date Line
- (C) talk about the Pacific Ocean and imaginary lines
- (D) remind you to wear a watch when flying

Name: ______________________________ Date: ______________

Directions: Read the text, and answer the questions.

Write one clarifying question you have about the text in the margin.

Time Zones

Long ago, each small community had a different way of using the sun to keep track of time. When people began to use trains, this became a problem. There was no good way to make a train schedule. Each community kept time in a different way, so it could be very confusing.

Sir Sandford Fleming was a Canadian railroad planner. He came up with a solution to this problem. His idea was a system of time zones that everyone would use. Each town's time zone would depend on where it was located. In 1884, people from 27 countries had a meeting in Washington, DC. They decided where those time zones would be.

Now, the world is divided into 24 time zones. There is no more confusion. It is easy to know what time it will be when you get to a new place.

1. *Came up with* means _____.
   - (A) did not like
   - (B) could not think of
   - (C) thought of
   - (D) asked for

2. The root word in *countries* is _____.
   - (A) count
   - (B) country
   - (C) county
   - (D) none of the above

3. Why did people need a precise way to keep time?

____

____

4. After reading the first sentence, what are two things a reader might predict the text will be about?

____

____

Name: ______________________________ Date: ________________

Write one clarifying question you have about the text in the margin.

What Time Is It?

Today, cars, trains, and airplanes go all over the world, crossing every time zone. There are 24 standard time zones in the world. Those zones are divided by time zone lines. Time zone lines are imaginary, like the International Date Line, so you cannot see them when you cross them. But they separate one time zone from the next. Time zone lines run from north to south. Places that are in the same time zone have the same time. Even places that are far away from each other might have the same time if they are in the same time zone. For example, Mexico City is in Mexico, and Winnipeg is in Canada. These countries are very far apart. But it's the same time in Mexico City as it is in Winnipeg because they are in the same time zone.

Many places change their clocks twice a year. In the spring, clocks are moved forward by one hour. This is known as daylight saving time. In the autumn, people set their clocks back again to standard time. People do this because in many parts of the world, days get longer during the summer. Setting clocks ahead allows people to have more daylight at the end of the day.

This chart shows the time in places around the world when it is noon on a Thursday in Los Angeles during daylight savings.

City, Country	Day	Time
Los Angeles, United States	Thursday	12:00 p.m.
Mexico City, Mexico	Thursday	2:00 p.m.
New York, United States	Thursday	3:00 p.m.
La Paz, Bolivia	Thursday	4:00 p.m.
London, England	Thursday	8:00 p.m.
Cairo, Egypt	Thursday	10:00 p.m.
Moscow, Russia	Thursday	11:00 p.m.
Auckland, New Zealand	Friday	9:00 a.m.

Name: ______________________________ Date: ________________

Directions: Read "What Time Is It?" Then, answer the questions.

1. What does the chart at the end of the article show?
   - (A) only cities in North America
   - (B) a train schedule
   - (C) the times at different locations
   - (D) a calendar

2. When are clocks moved forward an hour?
   - (A) in the spring
   - (B) at standard time
   - (C) in the winter
   - (D) on Thursdays

3. What is the main idea?
   - (A) Airplanes travel all over the world.
   - (B) It is Thursday in Mexico City.
   - (C) Daylight savings time happens in the spring.
   - (D) There are 24 standard time zones.

4. From the chart, it is ______ in Cairo than it is in London.
   - (A) later
   - (B) cooler
   - (C) earlier
   - (D) sooner

5. Write four facts about time zones.

Time Zones

Name: ______________________________ Date: ________________

Directions: Reread "What Time Is It?" Then, respond to the prompt.

Imagine you are a pilot. You enter different time zones as you fly from country to country. Write a paragraph to explain what might be hard about this. Share what might be fun about it. Use your imagination and information you learned to write your response.

Name: ______________________________ **Date:** ________________

Directions: Read the text, and answer the questions.

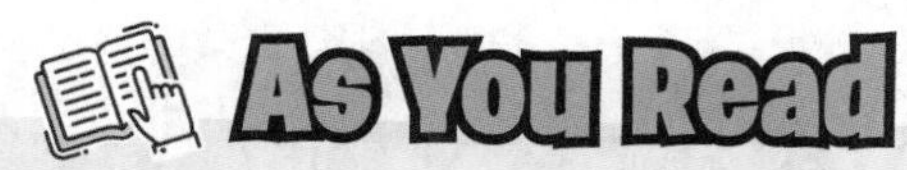

Underline important events in the story.

Time Traveler

Louis was on board a ship traveling east across the Pacific Ocean. It was sailing to San Francisco. He was traveling with his parents on a cruise that had toured China, Japan, and the Philippines. From San Francisco, his family would head home to Seattle.

Louis was feeling a little seasick, so he walked to an upper deck for fresh air. His ship was approaching the International Date Line. The date line cut between two small islands. One was owned by Russia, and the other was owned by the United States. After the ship passed the Russian island, its prow sliced across the date line. Louis's mom had told him that crossing the date line going east meant that you lose one day.

Awesome! thought Louis. *It's like going back in time.*

1. What is the root word of *awesome*?
   - (A) awes
   - (B) awe
   - (C) some
   - (D) me

2. What type of words are *small* and *large*?
   - (A) synonyms
   - (B) antonyms
   - (C) homophones
   - (D) alliteration

3. Why does Louis go to an upper deck?
   - (A) He feels seasick and wants fresh air.
   - (B) He wants to see the rest of the ship.
   - (C) He knows it is time to cross the International Date Line.
   - (D) His mom wants him to time travel.

4. Which sentence is true?
   - (A) Louis crossed over the International Date Line on his cruise.
   - (B) Louis went on a cruise throughout China, Japan, and Vietnam.
   - (C) Louis went to the future when he crossed between islands.
   - (D) China and the U.S. own islands between the International Date Line.

Name: ______________________ Date: ______________

Directions: Read the text, and answer the questions.

Underline important events in the story.

Crossing the Date Line

As the ship crossed the International Date Line, things faded from Louis's sight! He felt confused, like he was waking up from a bad dream. Louis stared around in shock. The cruise ship looked totally different. It was older and less sleek.

Louis went back inside the ship and saw people dressed in an old-fashioned way. Was this a costume party? He searched for his family's cabin, but there was no cabin with that number. Louis was starting to panic. He asked a crew member if they could help him find his family. But the crew member said no one in his family was listed as a passenger!

"Are you a stowaway?" he asked. "You'll have to come with me."

Louis turned and ran to the bow of the ship. Luckily, it had just docked in San Francisco. Louis darted down the gangplank and into the city. There were horse-drawn carriages everywhere and pedestrians were wearing old-fashioned clothes. What was going on?

1. What does *bow* mean in this text?

- (A) bending at the waist
- (B) the front of a ship
- (C) a tool used to play a violin
- (D) a knot made by tying string

2. What inference can you make about what happens in the text?

- (A) Louis's ship sank.
- (B) Louis's mom is playing a prank on him.
- (C) Louis traveled back in time.
- (D) Louis's ship is in distress.

3. What is the root word of *totally*?

- (A) *–ly*
- (B) totall
- (C) *–lly*
- (D) total

4. What is a *stowaway*?

- (A) a person who sneaks on a ship
- (B) a person who is invited on a cruise ship
- (C) a person who swims in the ocean
- (D) a person who is wearing a costume

Name: ______________________________ Date: ______________

Directions: Read the text, and answer the questions.

Underline important events in the story.

Welcome to San Francisco

Louis walked nervously up a street. He didn't know where he was going. He pulled out his cell phone to call his parents, but there was no reception. He jogged up a tall hill, hoping to get a signal, but there was still no reception.

Gazing at the famous San Francisco Bay in the distance, Louis realized something was missing. There was no Golden Gate Bridge! Fear gripped his stomach. Louis passed a newsstand and read the date on the paper: April 17, 1906. He had traveled back in time! He didn't lose just one day crossing the date line, he lost more than a century!

Louis knew his history, and this date shook him. On April 18, an earthquake would destroy a lot of San Francisco. It killed thousands of people, and hundreds of thousands of people were left without homes. He had to warn everyone that they were in great danger!

1. What is a synonym for *shook* as used in the text?
   - (A) swam
   - (B) jumped
   - (C) scared
   - (D) surprised

2. How should *reception* be broken into syllables?
   - (A) re·cep·tion
   - (B) rec·ep·tion
   - (C) re·cept·ion
   - (D) rec·ept·ion

3. Before seeing the newspaper date, what clues told you that Louis was in the past?

____

____

4. How could Louis help prepare people for the earthquake?

____

____

Name: ______________________ Date: ______________

Underline important events in the story.

Escaping the Quake

Louis started yelling to people on the street, "There's going to be an earthquake tomorrow! You need to leave the city!"

Some people laughed at him, and some were annoyed. One woman said, "Look at your strange clothes. Where are you from?" She had never seen a kid in sneakers and a T-shirt.

Louis became frantic, screaming his warnings as he ran.

A police officer walked over to Louis and asked, "Where are your folks?"

Louis replied, "They're on a ship in the Pacific Ocean."

The officer said, "You'd better come with me."

Louis tried to run away, but the officer grabbed his arm.

"We'll put you somewhere safe until we hear from your folks," the officer said. He took Louis to police headquarters to stay overnight. Louis sighed and tried to come up with a plan. What could he do now about the earthquake?

Around 4:30 the next morning, during a shift change, Louis snuck out. He didn't remember the exact time of the earthquake, but he knew it would happen soon. He needed to get away from the city center.

Louis walked towards the port, but a little after five in the morning, a police officer stopped him and said, "You're the kid from the station. Gotcha!"

But as he reached for Louis, the street began to shake. The officer fell to the ground and Louis took off running. A minute later, the main quake struck. The streets trembled and buckled, and big gaps opened in the sidewalk. Buildings swayed and started to collapse as Louis sprinted toward the harbor, scrambling to avoid debris. Soon, fires from broken gas lines began to spread. When Louis reached the docks, a sailor on a freighter waved him aboard.

"You'll be safe here," the sailor said. *His ship is bound for Hong Kong. That means it will cross the date line going west*, thought Louis. He hoped going the opposite way would take him home.

A week later, when the ship steamed past the date line, Louis felt woozy again. When he opened his eyes, he was back on his ship, heading back to modern San Francisco. *No one is going to believe what happened*, he thought.

Name: ______________________________ Date: ______________

Directions: Read "Escaping the Quake." Then, answer the questions.

1. Which is an antonym of *annoyed*?

- (A) angry
- (B) pleased
- (C) helpful
- (D) sad

2. How does Louis try to warn people about the earthquake?

- (A) making an announcement on the town square
- (B) going on television
- (C) telling the police
- (D) shouting to people on the street

3. Why does Louis travel to Hong Kong on the ship?

- (A) He would be safe from the earthquake.
- (B) He would cross the International Date Line.
- (C) The sailor kidnapped him.
- (D) The sailor believed his story.

4. Which word has a suffix?

- (A) quietly
- (B) earthquake
- (C) present
- (D) maybe

5. Write four important events from the story.

1.	
2.	
3.	
4.	

Name: ______________________ Date: ______________

Directions: Reread "Escaping the Quake." Then, respond to the prompt.

Louis tries to warn the people by shouting on the streets, and it doesn't work out very well. Rewrite the story with Louis warning them a different way. Be sure your story explains how Louis warns people and how the people react. End with the earthquake happening.

THE NATIONAL DAILY

Saving Standard Time

Twice a year, we have to reset our clocks. In the spring, we move the clock ahead one hour. We get one less hour of sleep, but we get one extra hour of sunlight. This is called Daylight Saving Time (DST). In the fall, we set the clocks back one hour. We get one more hour of sleep, but we get one less hour of sunlight. This is called Standard Time (ST). As a reminder, people say we "spring forward" and "fall back."

Not everyone likes to reset their clocks. Many people prefer the "spring forward" part but not the "fall back" part. They don't want to go back to Standard Time. That's why people are considering ending Standard Time. But is that a good idea? Here are the talking points people are using for and against DST.

Pro DST Arguments

- DST gives us longer daylight hours. More daylight keeps people safer. Motorists get into fewer accidents and are less likely to hit pedestrians. It's safer for children to play outside and for people to jog and walk their dogs in the evening.

- DST is good for the nation's economy. More people are outside during the extra daylight. They shop more. They drive more, which increases gas sales. In general, people spend more money during DST.

- DST is good for people's health. People spend more time exercising outside in the extra daylight.

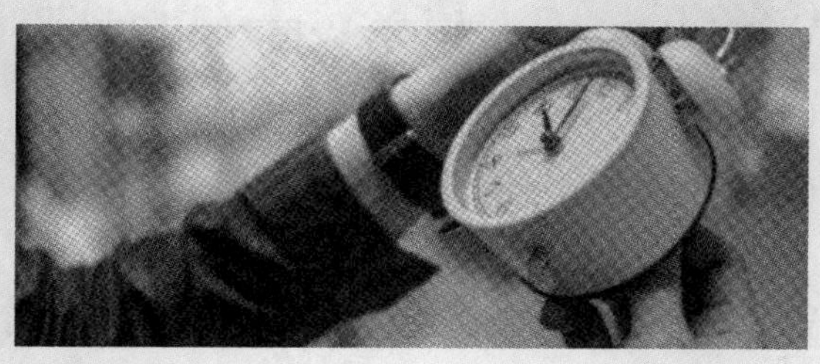

The Cons of DST

- In fact, DST isn't good for people's health. It's unnatural to have less light in the morning and more light in the evening. This upsets our internal body clocks, which are better set up with ST. Permanent DST could harm our thinking and immune systems, and it could even harm the health of our organs.

- Extra light in the evening makes it more difficult to get a good night's sleep. Not getting enough sleep can cause many different types of diseases.

- One reason we have DST is to save energy. But research shows there is almost no savings of electricity during DST.

Our Opinion

We think more debate around this issue is needed. The fact is, 43 percent of people polled want permanent ST. Only 32 percent want DST. Because of the health concerns of experts, we think it makes sense to keep ST and do away with DST.

We would like to know what our readers think. Send your opinion to our editorial department.

Name: ______________________________ Date: ______________

Directions: Read the editorial page from *The National Daily.* Then, answer the questions.

1. When does Standard Time begin?

Ⓐ summer
Ⓑ fall
Ⓒ winter
Ⓓ spring

2. What type of writing is an editorial?

Ⓐ persuasive
Ⓑ narrative
Ⓒ expository
Ⓓ advertisement

3. Why does the editorial state Standard Time should be kept?

Ⓐ It gives people more time to exercise in daylight hours.
Ⓑ It is good for the economy because people have longer to shop.
Ⓒ It is better for people's health and sleep habits.
Ⓓ It is better for gardening.

4. Which word has four syllables?

Ⓐ department
Ⓑ editorial
Ⓒ natural
Ⓓ pedestrian

5. What is one pro of keeping Daylight Saving Time?

____

____

____

Name: ______________________________ Date: ________________

Directions: Closely read these texts. Write information about the International Date Line given in each text.

Close-Reading Texts

International Date Line	Time Traveler
The answer is the International Date Line. The International Date Line is an imaginary line like the equator. It runs from north to south through the Pacific Ocean, and this line divides one day from the next day. So if it is Wednesday on the east side of the line, it is Thursday on the west side.	His ship was approaching the International Date Line. The date line cut between two small islands. One was owned by Russia, and the other was owned by the United States. After the ship passed the Russian island, its prow sliced across the date line. Louis's mom had told him that crossing the date line going east meant that you lose one day. *Awesome!* thought Louis. *It's like going back in time.*

International Date Line	Time Traveler

Name: ________________________________ Date: ________________

Directions: Closely read these texts. Compare and contrast the texts. Think about things such as genre, main topics or ideas, and language.

Close-Reading Texts

What Time Is It?	Escaping the Quake
There are 24 standard time zones in the world. Those zones are divided by time zone lines. Time zone lines are imaginary, like the International Date Line, so you cannot see them when you cross them. But they separate one time zone from the next. Time zone lines run from north to south. Places that are in the same time zone have the same time. Even places that are far away from each other might have the same time if they are in the same time zone.	*His ship is bound for Hong Kong. That means it will cross the date line going west,* thought Louis. He hoped going the opposite way would return him to his present time. A week later, when the ship steamed past the date line, Louis felt woozy again. When he opened his eyes, he was back on his ship, heading back to modern San Francisco.

What Time Is It? **Escaping the Quake**

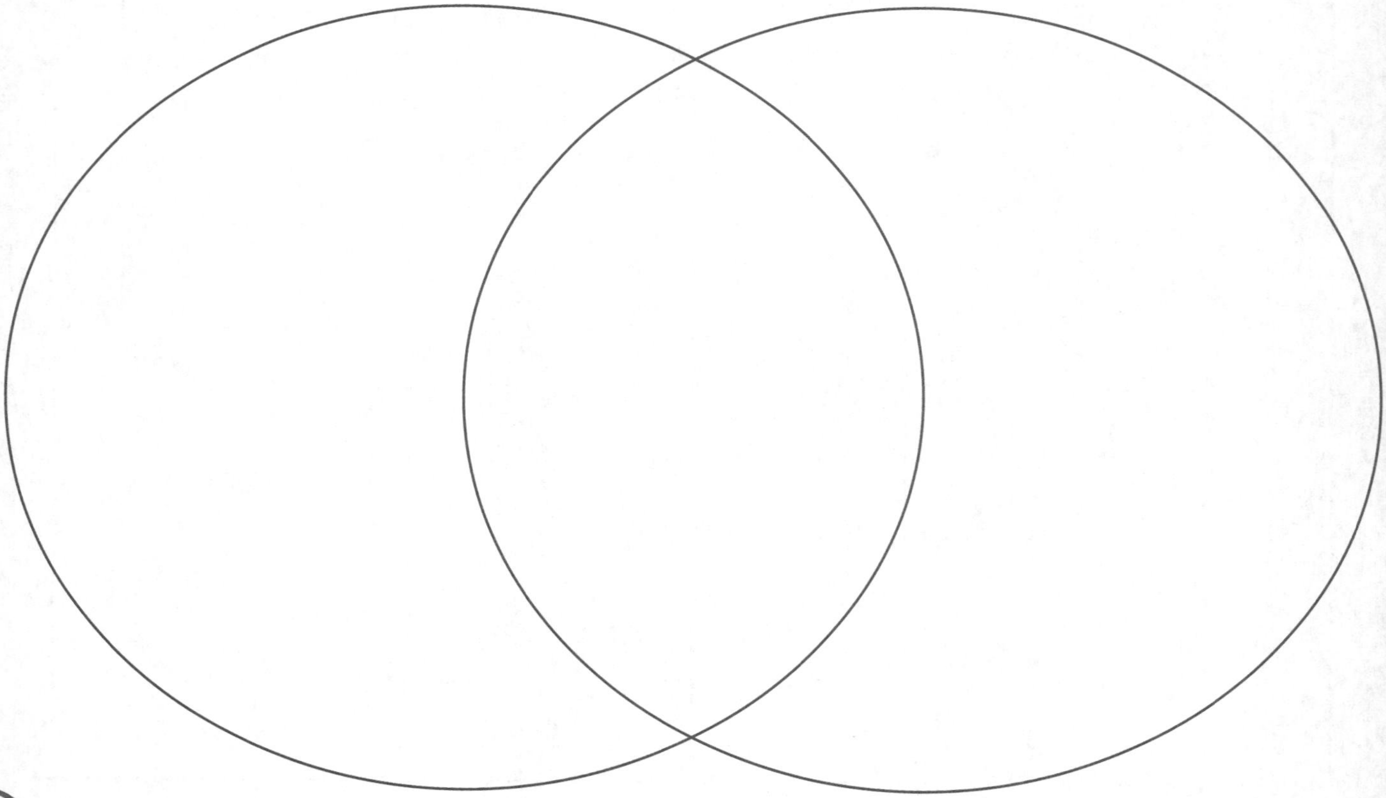

Name: ______________________________ Date: ______________

Directions: Reread "Saving Standard Time." Then, respond to the prompt.

Write your own letter to the editor in response to the stance that Standard Time should be permanent. Your letter should state whether you agree or disagree with the editorial's stance. It should also have at least two supporting reasons.

Name: ______________________________ **Date:** ________________

Directions: Think of an issue that has two sides. Then, write an editorial about the topic using the prompts.

The Issue: Give a brief explanation of the issue.

____

____

____

____

____

____

____

List the PROS

- ____
- ____

List the CONS

- ____
- ____

Your Opinion: Summarize your opinion with supporting reasons.

____

____

____

____

____

____

____

Name: ______________________________ Date: ______________

Directions: Read the text, and answer the questions.

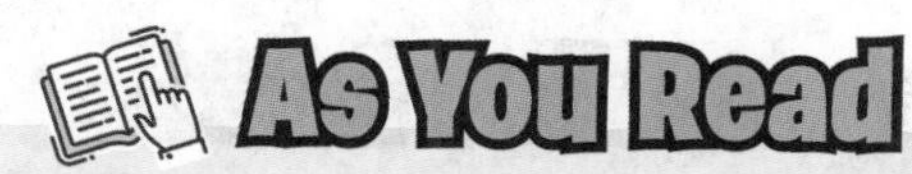

Circle important vocabulary words.

A Disappearing Act

Dinosaurs ruled the world for about 160 million years. That is a very long time. Humans have been around for only about 130,000 years! Scientists have found a lot of dinosaur bones in the earth. You have probably seen some in museums. Or maybe you have seen pictures of them in books.

About 65 million years ago, something puzzling took place. All the dinosaurs disappeared. They became extinct. Scientists are not sure what happened. It is hard to find out exactly why they disappeared. Scientists have many ideas.

Dinosaurs like *T.rex* do not exist anymore. But you may be surprised to hear that some animals are related to them. Can you guess what they are? They're birds!

1. How can scientists learn about dinosaurs?
   - (A) dinosaur photographs
   - (B) birds
   - (C) dinosaur bones
   - (D) extinct plants

2. What does the word *puzzling* mean in this text?
   - (A) fitting pieces together to create an image
   - (B) finding dinosaur bones in the ground
   - (C) confusing or not understood
   - (D) dangerous

3. What prefix is in the word *disappeared*?
   - (A) *di–*
   - (B) *–ed*
   - (C) *–ear*
   - (D) *dis–*

4. According to the text, how long have humans lived on Earth?
   - (A) 130,000 years
   - (B) 65 million years
   - (C) 160 million years
   - (D) 65,000 years

Name: ______________________________ Date: ________________

Directions: Read the text, and answer the questions.

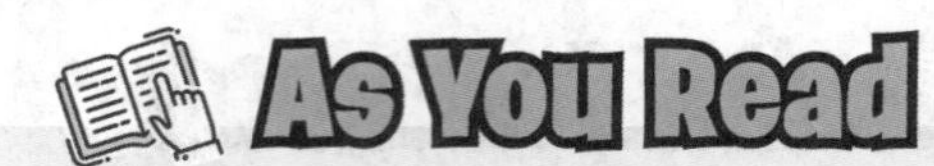

Circle important vocabulary words.

Many Theories

There are lots of theories on why dinosaurs died out. One scientist said caterpillars ate all the plants. So, the dinosaurs slowly starved. Some scientists believe a star exploded. It sent deadly radiation to Earth. There are even some wacky ideas out there. Some people think aliens somehow got rid of them.

Today, scientists have more convincing theories. One theory is that volcanoes killed the dinosaurs. Many huge volcanoes may have erupted at the same time. The lava could have killed them. Or they could have given off poisonous gas. Another theory says that sea levels dropped. There was less water on Earth. This changed the land and climate. And dinosaurs could not survive the changes.

Of all these theories, most scientists blame an asteroid. These large rocks circle the sun. This theory says that one of these rocks hit Earth 65 million years ago. It caused great destruction. One result was the death of the dinosaurs.

1. Which word means an idea meant to explain an event?
   - (A) extinct
   - (B) erupt
   - (C) destruction
   - (D) theory

2. How do most scientists think dinosaurs became extinct?
   - (A) poisonous gas from volcano eruptions
   - (B) caterpillars ate the plants
   - (C) asteroid hit the Earth
   - (D) dropping sea levels

3. What is the author's purpose?
   - (A) to inform readers about different extinction theories
   - (B) to persuade readers how dinosaurs became extinct
   - (C) to entertain readers with a funny story about dinosaurs
   - (D) to inform readers about asteroids and aliens

4. Which two words are synonyms?
   - (A) *erupt* and *explode*
   - (B) *erupt* and *poison*
   - (C) *starve* and *radiation*
   - (D) *convincing* and *result*

Name: ______________________________ Date: ______________

Directions: Read the text, and answer the questions.

Circle important vocabulary words. Write their definitions or synonyms in the margins.

Killer Rock

Walter Alvarez is an American geologist. He is an expert on the earth's structure. In 1980, he was studying a layer of dirt. The dirt contained a rare substance called *iridium*. This is found mostly in asteroids. Alvarez tested it. It turned out to be 65 million years old! Scientists in other countries also found the iridium in the ground. So, Alvarez came up with a theory. He said an asteroid hit the Earth long ago. Dust from the asteroid flew up and then fell back to Earth. This dust contained iridium. It formed a layer throughout the earth. Alvarez also thought the space rock probably made a big crater. He was not sure where. So he searched for it. And he found it! Alvarez discovered it in Mexico.

1. What is unusual about iridium?
   - (A) It is poisonous.
   - (B) It is a dust.
   - (C) It is found in asteroids.
   - (D) It is not real.

2. Which word is a compound word?
   - (A) substance
   - (B) throughout
   - (C) discovered
   - (D) peninsula

3. Why was the age of the iridium dust important?

____

____

____

4. How might dust from an asteroid have caused dinosaur extinction?

____

____

____

Unit 12
WEEK 1
DAY
4–5

Name: ______________________________ Date: ________________

Circle important content words.

The End of the Dinosaurs

It was just another day for *T. rex* and millions of other dinosaurs. They didn't know their world was about to end. Geologist Walter Alvarez has described what he thinks happened that day.

As the dinosaurs went about their business, a giant asteroid entered Earth's atmosphere. This was no ordinary space rock. It was about 6 miles (10 kilometers) in size. That's about as big as the city of San Francisco! The rock was moving 30,000 miles (48,280 km) a second. This is about 150 times faster than an airplane. As the rock cut through Earth's atmosphere, it squeezed the air in front of it. The air grew hotter than the sun. Some dinosaurs might have looked up at the strange light in the sky. When the rock hit the ground, it produced an enormous amount of energy. A shock wave went deep in the ground. A large portion of the earth shook. Then, the shock wave bounced back and vaporized the asteroid. This caused a fireball to rise high in the sky. It sent hot gases into outer space. Within moments, flying rock covered the ground for more than 60 miles (100 km). Every living thing in that area died instantly.

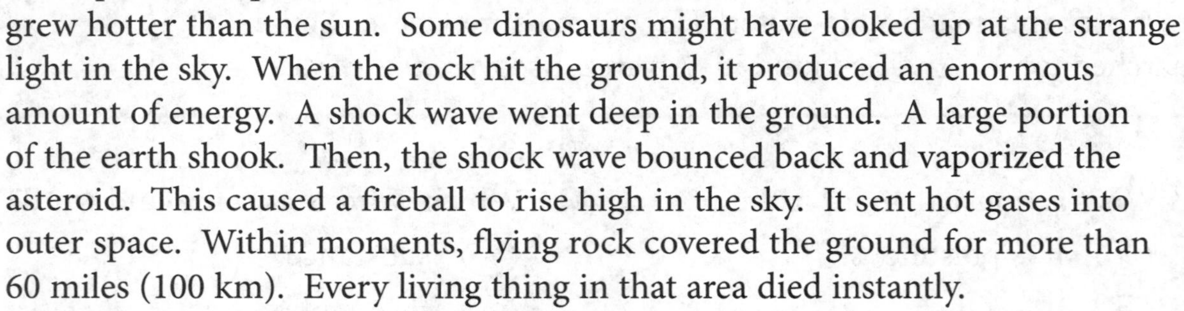

When the space rock landed, it made a huge crater. It was 25 miles (40 km) deep and almost 125 miles (200 km) wide. The force caused a giant wave called a *tsunami*. About 0.5 miles (1 km) high, it raced along the Gulf of Mexico and went inland, crushing forests and drowning dinosaurs. Worse, the collision threw hot rocks high in the sky. As the pieces came down, friction caused them to heat the air. The sky looked red. The air and ground became as hot as an oven. Animals died, and trees caught fire. Then, soot from the burning trees and dust from the explosion turned the sky black. Sunlight was blocked, and the temperature dropped. This left Earth cold and dark for months. Plants couldn't live without sunlight, so plant-eating dinosaurs starved. Dinosaurs that ate those dinosaurs starved as well.

Things got worse. The impact released lots of carbon dioxide into the air. This gas stayed trapped in the air, and it made Earth hot for thousands of years. Acid rain fell, harming marine life. In total, the asteroid ended up destroying about three-quarters of all species.

Name: ______________________ Date: ______________

Directions: Read "The End of the Dinosaurs." Then, answer the questions.

1. Which event happened right after the asteroid entered Earth's atmosphere?
   - (A) A tsunami moved inland.
   - (B) The air around it became hot.
   - (C) Carbon dioxide heated Earth's temperatures.
   - (D) An earthquake shook the ground.

2. What is a tsunami?
   - (A) a hot rock
   - (B) a poisonous gas
   - (C) a giant wave
   - (D) a large rock

3. Which is an antonym of *shallow*?
   - (A) narrow
   - (B) thoughtful
   - (C) large
   - (D) deep

4. Which word does **not** have three syllables?
   - (A) temperature
   - (B) collision
   - (C) asteroid
   - (D) destroying

5. Write two specific examples of cause and effect found in the text.

Cause	**Effect**
Cause	**Effect**

Name: ______________________________ Date: ________________

Directions: Reread "The End of the Dinosaurs." Then, respond to the prompt.

Imagine you are a time-traveling reporter. You safely witnessed the asteroid hitting Earth 65 million years ago. Write a newspaper article describing the events of the day. Remember, articles have a title and answer factual questions like *Who? What? When? Where? Why?* and *How?*

Name: ______________________________ Date: ______________

Directions: Read the text, and answer the questions.

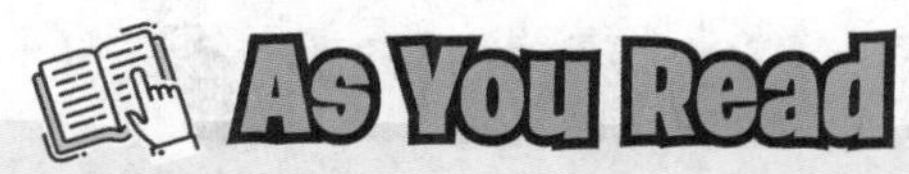

Put a star by at least one text-to-world connections you can make to the text.

At the Museum

"These bones are 80 million years old!" Elle shouted to her friend, Sarah. They were visiting the dinosaur hall in the science museum. Checking out an *Allosaurus* skeleton, Elle asked Sarah, "Where did they find these bones?"

Sarah said, "This sign says a paleontologist dug them up in Wyoming. What's a paleontologist?"

Elle was obsessed with dinosaurs, and she really knew her stuff.

"That's a scientist who studies life in prehistoric times," she said. "I wish I could go on a dig with a paleontologist."

"Your wish might come true," Sarah said, pointing at a notice.

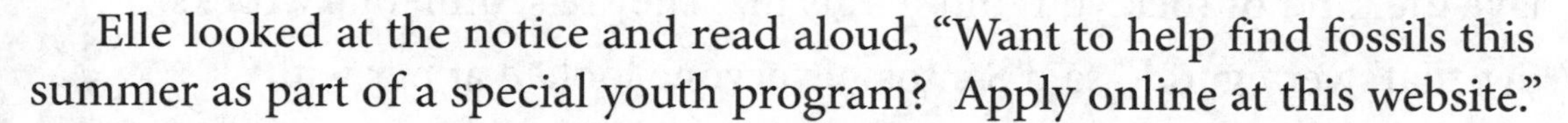

Elle looked at the notice and read aloud, "Want to help find fossils this summer as part of a special youth program? Apply online at this website."

Elle wrote down the address with a smirk.

1. How does Elle know what *paleontologist* means?

- (A) She read it on the sign.
- (B) She is interested in the topic.
- (C) Sarah told her.
- (D) It was a vocabulary word.

2. What does *notice* mean in the text?

- (A) to become aware of something by seeing it
- (B) to get attention for something
- (C) a warning that something is about to happen
- (D) a written paper that shares information

3. How should *prehistoric* be broken into syllables?

- (A) pre·hist·or·ic
- (B) pr·e·his·tor·ic
- (C) pre·hist·o·ric
- (D) pre·his·tor·ic

4. What inference can you make?

- (A) Elle will apply for the program.
- (B) Sarah will apply for the program.
- (C) The program is at the museum.
- (D) The program is only for boys.

Name: ______________________ Date: ______________

Directions: Read the text, and answer the questions.

Put a star by at least one text-to-world connections you can make to the text.

Off to Montana

That afternoon, Elle applied for the dinosaur dig. A few days later, she received an email. She had been accepted! She met Professor Earnest Santos, the leader of the expedition, in St. Louis. He was a friendly man with a short beard. He joined Elle and four other specially chosen kids on a train for Wyoming. Four other paleontologists were with them, too. When they arrived, Elle and the rest of the group climbed into a truck.

"We're off to the Badlands," said Santos.

"Badlands sound dangerous," said a boy named Marcus.

Elle laughed. "Actually, Badlands are good—for finding dinosaur bones. They have the kind of rock you find fossils in. They're sedimentary rocks."

"Wow, that's very good," said Santos. Everyone looked at her with wide eyes.

After a while, the truck stopped in the Badlands.

1. Which word is a synonym for *expedition*?
   - (A) danger
   - (B) student
   - (C) climb
   - (D) journey

2. Which is the best summary?
   - (A) Elle answered all the leader's questions.
   - (B) The group rode a train from St. Louis to Wyoming.
   - (C) Marcus thought the Badlands were dangerous.
   - (D) Elle and others travel to find dinosaur bones.

3. What inference makes the most sense?
   - (A) They are all silly.
   - (B) They all like dinosaurs.
   - (C) They get along.
   - (D) They are from St. Louis.

4. Why are the Badlands good for finding dinosaur bones?
   - (A) There are sedimentary rocks.
   - (B) The weather is warm.
   - (C) The paleontologists have a camp there.
   - (D) There are large trees.

Name: ______________________ Date: ______________

Directions: Read the text, and answer the questions.

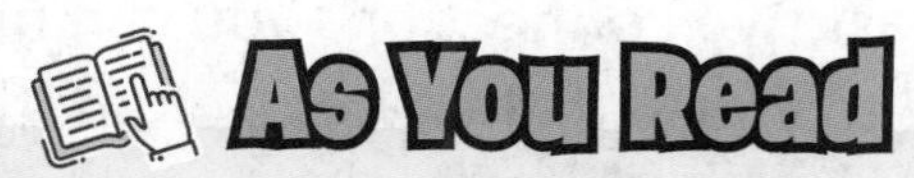

Put a star by at least one text-to-world connection you can make to the text.

A Big Discovery

Elle soon discovered that finding fossils was no easy task. Santos told her that it was best to look in areas where fossils had already been found.

"Plus, I have a knack for locating bones. It takes experience," he said. He pointed to one of the paleontologists. "Just follow Alicia and do what she says."

Alicia led Elle past some dry, steep slopes before stopping at the side of a hill.

Alicia said, "Let's start looking here, and if you see a fossil, call out to me."

Finding a fossil was much harder than Elle had expected. To her, a lot of rocks looked like fossils, but they weren't.

A couple hours later, Alicia and Elle hadn't found anything other than a rusted can. Suddenly, Alicia yelled in surprise, and Santos rushed over.

"It looks like an *Ankylosaurus* jawbone," Santos said. He brushed away some rock with one of his special tools. "Elle, please give Alicia a hand."

Elle rolled up her sleeves as a smile spread across her face.

1. Why is it hard for Elle to find a fossil?
   - (A) There aren't any there.
   - (B) They are in the wrong place.
   - (C) She needs her glasses.
   - (D) Rocks look like fossils.

2. What does Santos mean when he says he has a *knack for locating bones*?
   - (A) He is good at it.
   - (B) He is not very good at it.
   - (C) He has never done it before.
   - (D) He enjoys doing it.

3. According to Santos, where should they look for fossils?

____

4. What can you infer about how Elle feels at the end of the text?

____

Name: ______________________________ Date: ______________

Put a star by at least two connections you can make with the text. They can be to yourself, the world, or another text.

The Fantastic Fossil Find

Elle couldn't wait to start digging! The fossil was mostly buried in hard rock. Alicia took a heavy pick and began to gently remove rock. She handed Elle a small brush and told her to brush away from the fossil.

Elle tried to be as careful as she could, brushing the dust away from bone. But her hand accidentally slipped, and she scraped the bone.

"Careful!" Alicia said. Elle felt awful.

"No harm, no foul," said Alicia calmly. "It seems okay. Let's keep going."

Elle started to use the brush more carefully, and Alicia nodded her head in approval. She said, "Fossils are millions of years old, so they are super fragile."

Alicia took a plastic bottle and squeezed some liquid on the bone. She explained that the glue would harden the bone and keep it from fracturing. Then, Alicia took a small drill and cut away some rock along the sides of the fossil. Closer to the bone, she used a small dental pick. After more work, the bone and rock surrounding it were almost free.

Alicia said, "Now we put on a jacket."

"Isn't it kind of hot to wear a jacket?" asked Elle, squinting in the sun.

Laughing, Alicia said, "This jacket goes around the rock and the fossil. It keeps the bone secure."

"Oh, of course," said Elle, her face getting red.

Alicia first wrapped the bone and surrounding rock in wet paper towels. Then, she soaked strips of a rough cloth called burlap in wet plaster. Elle was about to help Alicia by placing the burlap over the paper towels, but she tripped and the wet burlap hit her face. Some plaster dripped down her nose.

She sighed and helped Alicia wrap the bone and rock with burlap. When they returned from lunch, the jacket was dry. They cut the jacket and lifted it onto a truck. Santos grinned and told them that the fossil would go to the museum with their other finds.

The next morning, Elle was searching at the bottom of a canyon when she saw something white. She called Santos over. He said, "You've found a raptor tooth. Well done! You have the makings of a future paleontologist!"

Name: ______________________ Date: ______________

Directions: Read "The Fantastic Fossil Find." Then, answer the questions.

1. Which best describes Elle's first day at the dig?

Ⓐ She makes a few mistakes.
Ⓑ She does not try very hard.
Ⓒ She does everything correctly.
Ⓓ She argues with others.

2. Why do fossils need jackets?

Ⓐ to keep them out of the light
Ⓑ to keep them warm
Ⓒ to keep them secure
Ⓓ to keep them dry

3. What is the root word of *easily*?

Ⓐ *–ly*
Ⓑ ease
Ⓒ easy
Ⓓ *–ily*

4. How should *digging* be broken into syllables?

Ⓐ di·gg·ing
Ⓑ dig·ging
Ⓒ digg·ing
Ⓓ di·gging

5. List four important events that happen in the story in the order they occur.

1.	
2.	
3.	
4.	

Name: ______________________________ Date: ______________

Directions: Reread "The Fantastic Fossil Find." Then, respond to the prompt.

Elle learns a lot her first day. Continue the story. Write about what happened on the second day. Think about what she might do, what problems she might encounter, and how she might deal with them. Include Alicia and Marcus in the story, too.

SCIENTIFIC NEWS WORLD

We bring science to everyone.

Home | Biology | Space | Earth | Archeology | Physics | Contact

Hit Or Miss?

Will an asteroid end life on Earth? Scientists hope to keep this from happening.

A giant space rock hit Earth 65 million years ago. It caused mass destruction. Could this happen again? Well, it has happened. Asteroids and meteors have hit Earth many times. More than 160 large craters have been found around the world. In fact, space rocks crash into Earth every day. Most are very small. But Earth has been hit by many large ones. Meteor Crater in Arizona is one of them. It was made 50 million years ago. In 1908, an asteroid exploded over a forest in Russia. It flattened millions of trees. In 2021, an asteroid came within 1.25 million miles of earth. That's only five times the distance of Earth to the moon. And here's more reason to worry: Nearly 30,000 asteroids orbit near Earth.

Scientists are trying to spot asteroids that might head our way. The rocks may be tiny dots in a telescope. But supercomputers are able to calculate if they will someday cross our path. Experts want to know an asteroid's size, shape, and speed. This helps them predict the damage it could cause if it were to hit our planet.

Can we stop asteroids from hitting Earth? In movies, atom bombs blow up asteroids to smithereens. In real life, asteroids are too heavy and fast to be destroyed that way. But a rocket hitting an asteroid might knock it slightly off course. Another idea is to send a large rocket close to the space rock. The rocket's gravity could change the asteroid's path away from Earth.

Above all, don't panic. Scientists don't think an asteroid will hit Earth in the next 100 years. Still, that won't stop scientists from keeping their eyes on the skies.

Name: ______________________ Date: ____________

Directions: Read the *Scientific News World* article. Then, answer the questions.

1. Which sentence from the first paragraph shares the main idea of the text?
   - (A) It caused mass destruction.
   - (B) Asteroids and meteors have hit Earth many times.
   - (C) Meteor Crater in Arizona is one of them.
   - (D) A giant space rock hit Earth 65 million years ago.

2. How many large craters have been found around Earth?
   - (A) almost 30,000
   - (B) over 160
   - (C) 1.25 million
   - (D) 1,908

3. If a reader wanted to learn about cells, which tab should they choose?
   - (A) Earth
   - (B) Space
   - (C) Physics
   - (D) Biology

4. What is the author's purpose for writing this web article?
   - (A) to persuade people to learn about craters
   - (B) to persuade people that they should be concerned
   - (C) to inform people how asteroids are formed
   - (D) to inform people about asteroids hitting Earth

5. Write the problem presented in the text and two possible solutions.

Problem

Solution

Solution

Name: ______________________________ Date: ________________

Directions: Closely read these texts. Then reread the web article on page 221. Write information shared about asteroids from each text.

Close-Reading Texts

Killer Rock	The End of the Dinosaurs
So, Alvarez came up with a theory. He said an asteroid hit the Earth long ago. Dust from the asteroid flew up and then fell back to Earth. This dust contained iridium. It formed a layer throughout the earth. Alvarez also thought the space rock probably made a big crater.	As the dinosaurs went about their business, a giant asteroid entered Earth's atmosphere. This was no ordinary space rock. It was about 6 miles (10 kilometers) in size. That's about as big as the city of San Francisco! The rock was moving 30,000 miles (48,280 km) a second. This is about 150 times faster than an airplane.

Killer Rock	
The End of the Dinosaurs	
Scientific News World **article**	

Name: ______________________________ Date: ______________

Directions: Closely read these texts. Think about the way the author discusses dinosaurs and their bones or fossils in each. Compare and contrast the information in the Venn diagram.

Close-Reading Texts

A Disappearing Act	The Fantastic Fossil Find
About 65 million years ago, something puzzling took place. All the dinosaurs disappeared. They became extinct. Scientists are not sure what happened. It is hard to find out exactly why they disappeared. Scientists have many ideas. Dinosaurs like *T.rex* do not exist anymore. But you may be surprised to hear that some animals are related them. Can you guess what they are? They're birds!	Alicia took a plastic bottle and squeezed some liquid on the bone. She explained that the glue would harden the bone and keep it from fracturing. Then, Alicia took a small drill and cut away some rock along the sides of the fossil. Closer to the bone, she used a small dental pick. After more work, the bone and rock surrounding it were almost free. Alicia said, "Now we put on a jacket."

A Disappearing Act **The Fantastic Fossil Find**

Name: ______________________ **Date:** ______________

Directions: Think about the texts from this unit. Then, respond to the prompt.

Imagine an asteroid is heading straight for Earth! You are the lead scientist on the team trying to stop impact. Write a short story about the event and your efforts to save the planet. Your story should have a beginning, middle, and end. It should be written in first-person.

Name: ______________________ Date: ______________

Directions: Create another article for the Scientific News World website. Think of a topic you are familiar with that fits one of the topics listed at the top. Write a paragraph about the topic. It should have introduction and conclusion sentences and at least three facts. Add an illustration to your site.

SCIENTIFIC NEWS WORLD

We bring science to everyone.

Home | Biology | Space | Earth | Archeology | Physics | Contact

Standards Correlations

Shell Education is committed to producing educational materials that are research and standards based. To support this effort, this resource is correlated to the academic standards of all 50 states, the District of Columbia, the Department of Defense Dependent Schools, and the Canadian provinces. A correlation is also provided for key professional educational organizations.

To print a customized correlation report for your state, visit our website at **www.tcmpub.com/administrators/correlations** and follow the online directions. If you require assistance in printing correlation reports, please contact the Customer Service Department at 1-800-858-7339.

Standards Overview

The Every Student Succeeds Act (ESSA) mandates that all states adopt challenging academic standards that help students meet the goal of college and career readiness. While many states already adopted academic standards prior to ESSA, the act continues to hold states accountable for detailed and comprehensive standards. Standardware is also used to develop standardized tests to evaluate students' academic progress. State standards are used in the development of our resources, so educators can be assured they meet state academic requirements.

College and Career Readiness

Today's college and career readiness (CCR) standards offer guidelines for preparing K–12 students with the knowledge and skills that are necessary to succeed in postsecondary job training and education. CCR standards include the Common Core State Standards as well as other state-adopted standards such as the Texas Essential Knowledge and Skills. The standards found in the digital resources describe the content presented throughout the lessons.

TESOL and WIDA Standards

English language development standards are integrated within each lesson to enable English learners to work toward proficiency in English while learning content–developing the skills and confidence in listening, speaking, reading, and writing. The standards found in the digital resources describe the language objectives presented throughout the lessons

Standards Correlations *(cont.)*

180 Days of Reading for Fourth Grade, 2nd Edition offers a full page of daily reading comprehension and word analysis practice activities for each day of the school year.

Every fourth grade unit provides questions and activities tied to a wide variety of language arts standards, providing students the opportunity for regular practice in reading comprehension, word recognition, and writing. The focus of the first two weeks in each unit alternates between nonfiction and fiction standards, with the third week focusing on both, as students read nontraditional texts and complete paired-text activities.

Reading Comprehension
Read and comprehend complex literary and informational texts independently and proficiently.
Read closely to determine what the text says explicitly. Ask and answer questions about the text and make logical inferences.
Determine central ideas or themes of a text and analyze their development; summarize the key supporting details and ideas.
Analyze how and why individuals, events, or ideas develop and interact over the course of a text.
Recognize and analyze genre-specific characteristics, structures, and purposes within and across diverse texts.
Use metacognitive skills to both develop and deepen comprehension of texts.
Analyze how two or more texts address similar themes or topics in order to build knowledge or to compare the approaches the authors take.
Assess how point of view or purpose shapes the content and style of texts.
Reading Foundational Skills
Know and apply grade-level phonics and word analysis skills in decoding words.
Language and Vocabulary Acquisition
Determine or clarify the meaning of unknown and multiple-meaning words and phrases by using context clues, analyzing meaningful word parts, and consulting general and specialized reference materials, as appropriate.
Demonstrate understanding of figurative language, word relationships, and nuances in word meanings.
Writing
Produce clear and coherent writing in which the development, organization, and style are appropriate to task, purpose, genre, and audience.
Respond to and draw evidence from literary or informational texts to show analysis, reflection, and research.

Writing Rubric

Score students' written responses using this rubric. Display the rubric for students to reference as they write. A student version of this rubric is provided in the digital resources.

Points	Criteria
4	• Uses an appropriate organizational sequence to produce very clear and coherent writing. • Uses descriptive language that develops or clarifies ideas. • Engages the reader. • Uses a style very appropriate to task, purpose, and audience.
3	• Uses an organizational sequence to produce clear and coherent writing. • Uses descriptive language that develops or clarifies ideas. • Engages the reader. • Uses a style appropriate to task, purpose, and audience.
2	• Uses an organizational sequence to produce somewhat clear and coherent writing. • Uses some descriptive language that develops or clarifies ideas. • Engages the reader in some way. • Uses a style somewhat appropriate to task, purpose, and audience.
1	• Does not use an organized sequence; the writing is not clear or coherent. • Uses little descriptive language to develop or clarify ideas. • Does not engage the reader. • Does not use a style appropriate to task, purpose, or audience.
0	• Offers no writing or does not respond to the assignment presented.

References Cited

Gough, Philip B., and William E. Tunmer. 1986. "Decoding, Reading, and Reading Disability." *Remedial and Special Education* 7 (1): 6–10.

Marzano, Robert. 2010. "When Practice Makes Perfect...Sense." *Educational Leadership* 68 (3): 81–83.

National Reading Panel. 2000. *Report of the National Reading Panel: Teaching Children to Read. Report of the Subgroups*. Washington, D.C.: U.S. Department of Health and Human Services, National Institutes of Health.

Scarborough, Hollis S. 2001. "Connecting Early Language and Literacy to Later Reading (Dis)abilities: Evidence, Theory, and Practice." In *Handbook of Early Literacy Research*, edited by Susan B. Neuman and David K. Dickinson, 97–110. New York: Guilford.

Soalt, Jennifer. 2005. "Bringing Together Fictional and Informational Texts to Improve Comprehension." *The Reading Teacher* 58 (7): 680–683.

Answer Key

Unit 1

Week 1

Day 1 (page 11)

1. B
2. B
3. A
4. C

Day 2 (page 12)

1. A
2. A
3. A
4. B

Day 3 (page 13)

1. B
2. A
3. The carapaces are shells that protect the turtles.
4. Sample response: People can clean up litter on the beach and leave the turtles and eggs alone.

Day 4 (page 15)

1. A
2. C
3. C
4. A
5. Venn diagrams should compare two sea animals with at least two differences and one similarity.

Day 5 (page 16)

Paragraphs should discuss the ways human endanger the animals, such as hunting and hitting the animals with boats. Ways people can help include: passing laws against hunting, using animal-safe hunting nets, and finding ways to keep animals away from boats.

Week 2

Day 1 (page 17)

1. A
2. D
3. D
4. B

Day 2 (page 18)

1. D
2. A
3. B
4. C

Day 3 (page 19)

1. C
2. B
3. Kyle can try out because his cast will be off and he likes to swim.
4. Sample response: I would tell Kyle to go on runs to build his stamina and watch videos about the different strokes.

Day 4 (page 21)

1. D
2. C
3. A
4. C
5. Kyle considers not trying out. His dad encourages him to try out. Kyle swims at the team try out. He asks the coach how he did. The coach tells Kyle he had one of the best times.

Day 5 (page 22)

Personal narratives should include additions to Kyle's story.

Week 3

Day 1 (page 24)

1. B
2. A
3. D
4. B
5. It means the anglerfish eats the fish that are attracted to its light. Answers should include a sentence using the phrase correctly.

Day 2 (page 25)

Sample response:

Title	Content word	Definition
Blue Whales: Ocean Giants	• krill • baleen	• small shrimp-like animals • a whale's teeth that help them eat krill
Making the Team	• plunged • churning	• jumped in • twisting and turning
Fantastic Fish!	• teem • venomous	• are full of • poisonous

Day 3 (page 26)

Sea turtles: reptiles; have shells

Manatees: mammals; have flat tails

Both: large, have flippers

Day 4 (page 27)

Articles should include information about three animals from the unit.

Day 5 (page 28)

Writing should include four facts about a topic of students' choosing.

Unit 2

Week 1

Day 1 (page 29)

1. A
2. A
3. D
4. C

Day 2 (page 30)

1. C
2. C
3. A
4. B

Day 3 (page 31)

1. C
2. D
3. The basenji doesn't bark, but it whines and yodels.
4. Sample response: The family should enjoy hiking and being outside because a basenji is an active dog and needs exercise.

Day 4 (page 33)

1. B
2. B
3. A
4. C
5. Student webs could include: space; activity level; family members; time.

Day 5 (page 34)

Letters should describe the space, time available, activity level, and family members for students' families, and suggest which type of dog will be a good match.

Week 2

Day 1 (page 35)

1. A
2. C
3. C
4. D

Answer Key (cont.)

Day 2 (page 36)

1. A
2. B
3. C
4. A

Day 3 (page 37)

1. B
2. D
3. Duke wouldn't eat the first few types of food Kim brought home.
4. Sample response: I think Kim is trying her best to be a good pet owner. She didn't realize how much work it would be to take care of a dog.

Day 4 (page 39)

1. D
2. D
3. C
4. A
5. Kim buys Duke a harness that is too loose. Duke slips out of the harness and is lost. Kim puts up missing dog flyers. A neighbor finds and returns Duke.

Day 5 (page 40)

Answers should rewrite important events from the story from Duke's point of view.

Week 3

Day 1 (page 42)

1. C
2. A
3. A
4. D
5. The boy loves his dog because he plays with it and tells it he loves it.

Day 2 (page 43)

Student webs should include ideas such as: train, feed, walk, groom, take to vet, play

Day 3 (page 44)

Basenjis—think for themselves, trained when young

Conversation with My Dog—fetch, sit

Both—do not bark back

Day 4 (page 45)

Short stories should describe the boy and dog having a conversation.

Day 5 (page 46)

Poems should include eight lines about an animal. Each two lines should rhyme.

Unit 3

Week 1

Day 1 (page 47)

1. D
2. C
3. C
4. A

Day 2 (page 48)

1. A
2. A
3. D
4. C

Day 3 (page 49)

1. C
2. C
3. A fire needs oxygen, fuel, and a heat source.
4. Sample response: I can keep towels away from the stove and not play with matches.

Day 4 (page 51)

1. D
2. C
3. D
4. A
5. practice as a team; learn new skills of putting out fires; learn to do first aid; exercise to stay in shape; clean their trucks and tools

Day 5 (page 52)

Paragraphs should explain if students would/would not want to be a firefighter using at least three supporting details from the text.

Week 2

Day 1 (page 53)

1. B
2. A
3. D
4. C

Day 2 (page 54)

1. B
2. B
3. B
4. A

Day 3 (page 55)

1. A
2. C
3. The fire drill at school causes Willa to think about the fire plan for her home.
4. Sample response: Willa's plan might be to go out the front door and meet in the neighbor's driveway. The family might need to go out a first-floor window.

Day 4 (page 57)

1. C
2. D
3. B
4. B
5. Answers should include completed tables comparing students to two characters from the story.

Day 5 (page 58)

Student plans should describe two ways to exit their home in case of a fire; plans should have accompanying maps.

Week 3

Day 1 (page 60)

1. D
2. A
3. A
4. D
5. Smoke jumpers cut down trees or dig ditches to make a line that stops the burning.

Day 2 (page 61)

Smoke Alarms	smoke alarms; call fire department; get to safety; test smoke alarms; change batteries
Finding Fire Hazards	burning leaves can spread fire; beanie over lamp; new batteries for smoke alarm
Sensational Smokejumpers	Put on protective gear; cut trees; create a fire line

Answer Key (cont.)

Day 3 (page 62)

	Purpose	Genre
How Fires Start	To inform	Nonfiction
House on Fire	To entertain	Fiction
Both		
Both are about fires.		

Day 4 (page 63)

Writing should include speeches explaining Willa's history with fire safety and describing her actions the night of her house fire.

Day 5 (page 64)

Writing should include captions for tasks of students' choice; drawings should accompany the steps.

Unit 4

Week 1

Day 1 (page 65)

1. D
2. C
3. A
4. C

Day 2 (page 66)

1. A
2. D
3. B
4. C

Day 3 (page 67)

1. D
2. C
3. A goal is scored when a player kicks the ball into the other team's goal.
4. Sample response: Players might run down the field holding the ball instead of kicking it.

Day 4 (page 69)

1. C
2. D
3. D
4. A
5.

Amazon River	It flows into the Atlantic Ocean.
Amazon Rain Forest	More than half of the world's plants and animals live there.
seasons	July is a winter month.
cities	The capital of Brazil is Brasilia.
football	Football is very popular.

Day 5 (page 70)

Student paragraphs should persuade readers to visit Brazil and use three details from the text to support their reasoning.

Week 2

Day 1 (page 71)

1. C
2. A
3. D
4. B

Day 2 (page 72)

1. D
2. A
3. C
4. B

Day 3 (page 73)

1. B
2. A
3. The climate is hot because Paulo swims year-round and wears summer clothes all of the time.
4. Answers should include questions students would like to ask Paulo.

Day 4 (page 75)

1. D
2. A
3. A
4. B
5. Beaches—Copacabana, Ipanema; City Sights—Tijuca National Park, Sugar Loaf Mountain, statue of Christ, museums; Food—feijoada, fruit juice, fried cod balls

Day 5 (page 76)

Letters to pen pals should include information about students and their home, as well as a few questions for the pen pals to answer.

Week 3

Day 1 (page 78)

1. D
2. C
3. B
4. C
5. People visit Brazil because it is a large, diverse country with warm temperatures and beautiful beaches.

Day 2 (page 79)

An Important Rain Forest	Rio Rocks!	Brazil
• The rainforest gets over 59 inches of rain a year • It is home to one-half of the world's species.	• The Copacabana is a famous beach. • *Cariocas* are people from Rio.	• Brazil is the fifth largest country in the world. • The capital is Brasilia. • It has a tropical climate.

Day 3 (page 80)

Welcome to Brazil—carnival, parades, parties, costumes

Rio Rocks—Tijuca National Park, Sugar Loaf Mountain, statue of Christ, museums

Both—beaches

Day 4 (page 81)

Paragraphs should contain information about Brazil and include introduction and conclusion sentences.

Day 5 (page 82)

Paragraphs should give information about the country, and the fact list should be filled out correctly.

Unit 5

Week 1

Day 1 (page 83)

1. B
2. C
3. B
4. D

Day 2 (page 84)

1. A
2. C
3. C
4. D

Answer Key *(cont.)*

Day 3 (page 85)

1. B
2. B
3. Pebbles become rounded when flowing water erodes and smooths them.
4. Sample response: Searching for water is a rover's most important job because finding water will help scientists learn if there was ever life on Mars.

Day 4 (page 87)

1. B
2. A
3. B
4. D
5. Spokes—young people will want to study math and science; people will be inspired; create new jobs and technology; look for signs of life; help live sustainably on Earth

Day 5 (page 88)

Summaries should be at least four sentences and summarize the most important details from the text.

Week 2

Day 1 (page 89)

1. B
2. A
3. D
4. C

Day 2 (page 90)

1. A
2. A
3. C
4. D

Day 3 (page 91)

1. C
2. C
3. Students don't learn Earth history.
4. Sample response: Josh could be bullied for being an Outerling; it might be hard to adjust to the new foods; he could struggle to learn new subjects.

Day 4 (page 93)

1. D
2. A
3. C
4. D
5. Characters—Josh, Cody, Demos, other students; Setting—Mars and an underground cavern on Mars; Plot—Josh and other Martians found a new place to explore on Mar's surface. They found an underground lake of water.

Day 5 (page 94)

Writing should explain who Josh is and how finding water helped life on Mars.

Week 3

Day 1 (page 96)

1. A
2. D
3. D
4. B
5. The problem is there is a huge dust storm approaching and the cops and climber might get stuck in the storm.

Day 2 (page 97)

Robots on Mars	rocky surface, dust storms, dry riverbeds, rounded pebbles
Landing on Mars	Deadly atmosphere
Mars Patrol	Dust storms, deep channels

Day 3 (page 98)

	Expedition to Mars	Landing on Mars
Length of Trip	500 days	Six months
Possible Dangers	Weak muscles and bones; emotional distress	Solar flares
	Both	
Traveling to Mars		

Day 4 (page 99)

Narratives should tell stories of the climber before he was rescued by patrol officers.

Day 5 (page 100)

Graphic novel frames should include text and drawings to continue the story.

Unit 6

Week 1

Day 1 (page 101)

1. B
2. C
3. D
4. A

Day 2 (page 102)

1. A
2. D
3. A
4. C

Day 3 (page 103)

1. A
2. B
3. You should bring a camera.
4. Sample response: You could research online or look in a book about the city's climate.

Day 4 (page 105)

1. C
2. C
3. A
4. D
5.

Staying on the Cruise Ship:	Getting off the Cruise Ship:
• Swim in a pool • Go mini golfing • Eat at a restaurant	• Explore the new place • Hike • Go shopping

Day 5 (page 106)

Postcards should be written as letters and include activities from the text students could participate in on cruises. They should also draw and color pictures for the front of the postcard.

Week 2

Day 1 (page 107)

1. B
2. D
3. C
4. A

Day 2 (page 108)

1. C
2. D
3. D
4. A

Answer Key *(cont.)*

Day 3 (page 109)

1. A
2. C
3. Sample response: Camping rules keep people safe. If people drank from a contaminated steam, they could get very sick.

Day 4 (page 111)

1. A
2. B
3. C
4. A
5.

Cause	Effect
Cara saw the waterfall.	She realized she was thirsty.
Cara kept walking south.	She made her way back to the trail and her campsite.

Day 5 (page 112)

Personal narratives should each have a beginning, middle, and end, and should explain why students changed their mind about something they originally did not like.

Week 3

Day 1 (page 114)

1. B
2. B
3. A
4. D
5. Road Trip Stops—Gateway Arch in St. Louis, Grand Canyon, Rock and Roll Hall of Fame in Cleveland, Wrigley Field in Chicago, ball of twine in Kansas

Day 2 (page 115)

Vacation Variety	Going Camping	Postcard
Hiking, camping, swimming, visiting museums and restaurants	Camping, hiking, beach	Hiking, swimming, road trip, visiting city landmarks

Day 3 (page 116)

Different: The first paragraph is nonfiction and describes how vacations are healthy because they help the body rest. The second is fiction and describes a girl's experience hiking.

Same: Both describe good things that can happen on vacation.

Day 4 (page 117)

Paragraphs should include reasons why the locations students chose would be good places for their families to go on vacations.

Day 5 (page 118)

Postcards should each describe a fun place students visited in their own city. They should also draw a picture for the front of the postcard.

Unit 7

Week 1

Day 1 (page 119)

1. D
2. B
3. D
4. D

Day 2 (page 120)

1. A
2. D
3. B
4. B

Day 3 (page 121)

1. C
2. D
3. When the arrow is shot, it makes the pattern of an arch in the air.
4. Sample response: A person would need to be strong, have a steady hand, and have good vision to be a skilled archer.

Day 4 (page 123)

1. D
2. B
3. B
4. C
5.

Paragraph 1	Archery is an old, but popular, sport.
Paragraph 2	Archery is good exercise for the body.
Paragraph 3	Most people are able to participate in archery.
Paragraph 4	People should follow the rules to be safe during archery

Day 5 (page 124)

Paragraphs should each explain a sport, hobby, or activity students enjoy, why they like it, and how other people can get involved.

Week 2

Day 1 (page 125)

1. B
2. D
3. B
4. A

Day 2 (page 126)

1. D
2. B
3. A
4. C

Day 3 (page 127)

1. B
2. A
3. Rory brags a lot. He says he's a superhero when his arrow hits the target and he tells Sophia he will win the contest easily.
4. Sample response: I predict Sophia will win the contest even though Rory brags he will.

Day 4 (page 129)

1. B
2. A
3. D
4. D
5. Sophia—talented, patient, hard worker, forgiving; Rory—boastful, competitive, sore loser, honest

Answer Key *(cont.)*

Day 5 (page 130)

Student writing should give an alternate ending telling what might have happened if the two main characters had finished in different places in the tournament.

Week 3

Day 1 (page 132)

1. C
2. D
3. A
4. A
5. Archery is an ancient sport and has been used in almost every civilization, and a person who loves history might be interested in it.

Day 2 (page 133)

Bow and Arrow History	Wood, stone
Getting Started	Compound, recurve, and traditional bows
Welcome to Archery!	Wood, plastic, or metal arrows

Day 3 (page 134)

Sample response:

An Arrow's Flight	**Getting Competitive**
• Nonfiction • Teaches that an arrow arches up and then gravity pulls it down	• Fiction • Sophia doesn't get her arrow to the bull's eye
Both • Shooting arrows	

Day 4 (page 135)

Writing should include dialogues between children and their parents about archery.

Day 5 (page 136)

Advertisements should describe lessons and give information about them. The ads should also include illustrations.

Unit 8

Week 1

Day 1 (page 137)

1. C
2. C
3. D
4. A

Day 2 (page 138)

1. B
2. C
3. D
4. A

Day 3 (page 139)

1. B
2. B
3. People thought the factories caused pollution and poverty, and they felt like life was becoming too stressful.
4. Sample response: People liked the book because it was about technology going too far, and they thought that was happening in real life, too.

Day 4 (page 141)

1. B
2. A
3. B
4. A
5. 1797—Shelley is born. 1801—Shelley's father remarries. 1813—Shelley gets married. 1816—Shelley travels with friends. 1818—*Frankenstein* is published. 1851—Shelley dies.

Day 5 (page 142)

Time lines should include years and descriptions for five life events.

Week 2

Day 1 (page 143)

1. D
2. A
3. B
4. C

Day 2 (page 144)

1. A
2. A
3. B
4. C

Day 3 (page 145)

1. D
2. D
3. Max is the director because making the movie was his idea.
4. Sample response: Max is good at solving problems because when he didn't have video equipment, he decided to use his phone instead.

Day 4 (page 147)

1. B
2. D
3. D
4. C
5.

Ella	Writing script
Brett	Creating lab set
Frankie	Spooky costumes
Cory	Lighting

Day 5 (page 148)

Paragraphs should be detailed character evaluations of Max using at least two character traits, such as ambitious and creative, and give examples from the text to support them.

Week 3

Day 1 (page 150)

1. C
2. A
3. A
4. D
5. The monster asks Victor to create him a girlfriend and fetch him something to eat. Victor second-guesses creating the monster.

Day 2 (page 151)

Fear of Change	Stressful lives, technology
My Favorite Monster	Sharks, clowns, movies, monsters
***Frankenstein* script**	Creating the monster

Day 3 (page 152)

People from 1800s—afraid of cars, electricity

Max—mad that his friends have better ideas

Both—afraid of things they don't know

Answer Key (cont.)

Day 4 (page 153)

Writing should include Max's acceptance speech for his movie award, and should include what he learned and who he should thank.

Day 5 (page 154)

Scripts should have two characters with at least six total lines of dialogue. There should also be descriptions of the settings and stage directions.

Unit 9

Week 1

Day 1 (page 155)

1. C
2. B
3. D
4. B

Day 2 (page 156)

1. C
2. B
3. A
4. D

Day 3 (page 157)

1. B
2. A
3. A person gets half their genes from their mother and half from their father.
4. Sample response: The person could have the eye color of the parent with the dominant eye color gene.

Day 4 (page 159)

1. C
2. A
3. A
4. D
5. pumpkins—round, orange, leaves; panda bears—black and white fur, black eyes, black ears; basset hounds—droopy ears, long body, good sense of smell

Day 5 (page 160)

Summaries should include important ideas from each of the passage's paragraphs.

Week 2

Day 1 (page 161)

1. A
2. B
3. C
4. C

Day 2 (page 162)

1. A
2. A
3. C
4. A

Day 3 (page 163)

1. D
2. B
3. Stefan's sister looks like her mom because they both have blue eyes and light, curly hair.
4. Sample response: Stefan will discover that they have some traits in common, but not as many as with his immediate family.

Day 4 (page 165)

1. D
2. B
3. C
4. A
5. asked his dad; talked to Uncle Joe; talked to Frank

Day 5 (page 166)

Answers should describe childhood events that could be shared in the future with young family members.

Week 3

Day 1 (page 168)

1. D
2. D
3. C
4. A
5. DNA is a chemical in a person's cells that makes up their genes. It tells a body how it should look and act.

Day 2 (page 169)

Text	Word 1 and Definition	Word 2 and Definition
Passing Down Genes	Genes—part of a cell that says what a thing looks like	Physical characteristics—the way a person looks
The Family Tree	Traits—a quality that makes one thing different from another	Exhibited—to show
It's All in the Genes	DNA—a chemical in cells that says what a person looks like	Experiment—scientific test to learn something new

Day 3 (page 170)

Sample response:

What do the paragraphs have in common?

Both paragraphs explain that genes come from both a mother and a father.

What different information do the paragraphs have?

The first paragraph explains specifically how eye color is passed from parent to child. The second paragraph gives examples of traits a brother and sister inherited from their parents.

Day 4 (page 171)

Answers should include a paragraph that describes at least three ways students are similar to or different from family members.

Day 5 (page 172)

Answers should each give the materials list, step-by-step directions, and end result for something students can give directions to do.

Answer Key *(cont.)*

Unit 10

Week 1

Day 1 (page 173)

1. C
2. B
3. A
4. A

Day 2 (page 174)

1. B
2. C
3. A
4. A

Day 3 (page 175)

1. A
2. C
3. Take shelter means to go somewhere safe.
4. Sample response: I would go into the basement bathroom because it is an inside room and also downstairs.

Day 4 (page 177)

1. D
2. A
3. D
4. A
5. Flow chart steps: check computer to find a storm; travel to the place; watch sky; take photos of weather.

Day 5 (page 178)

Journal entries should be written from the perspective of storm chasers and describe how they found storms and what happened.

Week 2

Day 1 (page 179)

1. A
2. B
3. C
4. B

Day 2 (page 180)

1. A
2. C
3. B
4. B

Day 3 (page 181)

1. B
2. B
3. Lisa likes the creek because she says it's beautiful and wants to have a picnic.
4. Sample response: Tricia might have invited Lisa because she wanted to experience a fun place with her friend.

Day 4 (page 183)

1. A
2. D
3. D
4. C
5. Problem: It begins raining at the girls' picnic. Solution: They pack up their belongings and go back to Tricia's house.

Day 5 (page 184)

Stories should continue where the passage left off and describe the girls' rainy afternoon together.

Week 3

Day 1 (page 186)

1. C
2. B
3. A
4. B
5. the tornado—started as a super cell, EF-4 rating, hail, pulling up trees, growing from ¼ to ½ mile across, lightning, louder than a jet plane, moving like a wall of black air

Day 2 (page 187)

Title	Storm Description
Dangerous Winds	weak, pulling dirt and leaves; strong and pulling trees and breaking windows
A Very Wet Picnic	Hard rain, booming thunder, dripping wet
Radio Transmission	Hailing, strong winds, thunder and lightning, pulling up a car

Day 3 (page 188)

Sample response:

Storm Chasers—nonfiction, traveling, general information

Radio Transmission—fiction, storm details (rating and speed)

Both—about storm chasers, recording storms

Day 4 (page 189)

Paragraphs should state students' opinions, give three supporting details, and have conclusion sentences.

Day 5 (page 190)

Answers should each include a script of a radio broadcast between two reporters about a news, sports, or event topic of their choice.

Unit 11

Week 1

Day 1 (page 191)

1. A
2. A
3. D
4. B

Day 2 (page 192)

1. C
2. A
3. B
4. B

Day 3 (page 193)

1. C
2. B
3. People needed to keep time because of train schedules.
4. Sample response: A reader could predict the paragraph will explain why time zones were needed and who thought of the idea.

Answer Key (cont.)

Day 4 (page 195)

1. C
2. A
3. D
4. A
5. time zones—24 around the world; lines are imaginary; lines run north and south; places in same time zone have the same time

Day 5 (page 196)

Answers should be from the perspective of a pilot and should explain what might be hard and fun about flying into different time zones.

Week 2

Day 1 (page 197)

1. B
2. B
3. A
4. A

Day 2 (page 198)

1. B
2. C
3. D
4. A

Day 3 (page 199)

1. C
2. A
3. Louis did not have cell phone reception and the Golden Gate Bridge was not built.
4. Sample response: Louis could go to City Hall and tell officials, take out an ad in the newspaper, shout it out on the streets, or do a radio announcement.

Day 4 (page 201)

1. B
2. D
3. B
4. A
5.

1.	Louis shouts on the street and tries to warn people about the earthquake.
2.	A police officer grabs Louis and puts him in jail.
3.	He escapes and goes on a ship in the harbor during the quake.
4.	The ship crosses the International Date Line and he is back in the present.

Day 5 (page 202)

Narratives should describe Louis warning people different ways about the earthquake, their reactions, and what happens during the quake.

Week 3

Day 1 (page 204)

1. B
2. A
3. C
4. D
5. Pros are: people stay out longer to shop and drive which is good for the economy; people can exercise outdoors later in the evening; people are safer and there are fewer car accidents.

Day 2 (page 205)

International Date Line—imaginary lines; runs north and south in the Pacific Ocean

Time Traveler—IDL cuts between two islands; going east loses one day

Day 3 (page 206)

Sample response:

What Time Is It?—nonfiction; informing about the IDL and time zones

Escaping the Quake—fiction; using IDL as magic

Both—about time zones and the International Date Line

Day 4 (page 207)

Letters should state if students agree or disagree with the editorial's stance on Standard Time. They should give two reasons to support their opinions.

Day 5 (page 208)

Editorials should explain issues, give pros and cons, and state opinions with reasoning.

Unit 12

Week 1

Day 1 (page 209)

1. C
2. C
3. D
4. A

Day 2 (page 210)

1. D
2. C
3. A
4. A

Day 3 (page 211)

1. C
2. B
3. The dust was 65 million years old, the same time dinosaurs became extinct.
4. Sample response: The dust could be poisonous; it could have killed plants and polluted water; it could have blocked sunlight.

Day 4 (page 213)

1. B
2. C
3. D
4. A
5.

Cause	Effect
Asteroid landed with great force.	A giant tsunami went inland and drowned dinosaurs.
Cause	**Effect**
Soot from fires made the sky dark.	Plants died without sunlight.

Day 5 (page 214)

Articles should describe the events that happened the day the asteroid hit Earth.

Week 2

Day 1 (page 215)

1. B
2. D
3. D
4. A

Day 2 (page 216)

1. D
2. D
3. B
4. A

Answer Key *(cont.)*

Day 3 (page 217)

1. D
2. A
3. They should look for bones where they have already found some.
4. Sample response: Elle feels excited because they found a dinosaur bone and that is what she has been hoping for the whole trip.

Day 4 (page 219)

1. A
2. C
3. B
4. B
5. Sample response:

1	Elle began brushing dust off the fossil.
2	Alicia wrapped the fossil in a jacket.
3	They removed the fossil from the hill and put it on the truck.
4	Elle found a raptor tooth.

Day 5 (page 220)

Narratives should continue the story on the second day of the dig. Alicia and Marcus should be included.

Week 3

Day 1 (page 222)

1. B
2. B
3. D
4. D
5. Problem: An asteroid might hit Earth.

   Solution: Send a rocket into space to hit the asteroid and bump it off course.

   Solution: Send a rocket into space close to the asteroid so its gravity changes the asteroid's course.

Day 2 (page 223)

Killer Rock	• Dust from the asteroid formed a layer on Earth • The dust had iridium in it.
The End of the Dinosaurs	• Asteroid was as large as San Francisco. • Asteroid moving 30,000 miles a second.
***Scientific News World* article**	• 30,000 asteroids orbit near Earth. • Over 160 large asteroids have left craters.

Day 3 (page 224)

A Disappearing Act—Dinosaurs disappeared 65 million years ago; Birds are related to dinosaurs.

The Fantastic Fossil Find—Special tools can separate dinosaur bone and rock; Glue hardens the dinosaur bones and keeps them from fracturing.

Both—dinosaur bones and fossils

Day 4 (page 225)

Narratives should be written in first person and be about saving the planet from an asteroid hitting Earth. They should each have a beginning, middle, and end.

Day 5 (page 226)

Paragraphs should share three facts about topics related to biology, space, Earth, archeology, or physics.

Digital Resources

Accessing the Digital Resources

The digital resources can be downloaded by following these steps:

1. Go to **www.tcmpub.com/digital**
2. Use the 13-digit ISBN number to redeem the digital resources.
3. Respond to the question using the book.
4. Follow the prompts on the Content Cloud website to sign in or create a new account.
5. The content redeemed will appear on your My Content screen. Click on the product to look through the digital resources. All file resources are available for download. Select files can be previewed, opened, and shared.

For questions and assistance with your ISBN redemption, please contact Shell Education.

email: customerservice@tcmpub.com

phone: 800-858-7339

Contents of the Digital Resources

- Standards Correlations
- Writing Rubric
- Fluency Rubric
- Class and Individual Analysis Sheets

